Map Attack!
UNDERSTANDING GLOBES AND MAPS

JACK WARNER

CAMBRIDGE   Adult Education
Prentice Hall Regents, Englewood Cliffs, NJ 07632

Executive editor: James W. Brown
Editorial Supervision: Timothy A. Foote
Production supervision and interior design: Noël
    Vreeland Carter
Cover design: Bruce Kenselaar
Cover art: William Lombardo, The Image Bank
Technical illustrations: Alice B. Thiede and William
    A. Thiede, Carto-Graphics
Art illustration: Don Martinetti
Pre-press buyer: Ray Keating
Manufacturing buyer: Lori Bulwin
Scheduler: Leslie Coward

ACKNOWLEDGEMENT

The author wishes to thank the following for their
contributions during the preparation of this book.

Judith B. Chandler, Ed.D., Media Producer
Univ. of Georgia, Georgia Center for Continuing
    Education

Lee Chic, Instructor
San Mateo County Community School South

Cliff Jenkins, Basic Skills Instructor
San Mateo County Office of Education

Lynne Porter, Curriculum Specialist
Los Angeles Unified School District Division of Adult
    and Occupational Education

©1991 by Prentice-Hall, Inc.
A Simon & Schuster Company
Englewood Cliffs, New Jersey 07632

Printed in the United States of America
10 9 8 7 6 5 4 3 2 1

0-13-962903-3

Prentice-Hall International (UK) Limited, *London*
Prentice-Hall of Australia Pty. Limited, *Sydney*
Prentice-Hall Canada Inc., *Toronto*
Prentice-Hall Hispanoamericana, S.A., *Mexico*
Prentice-Hall of India Private Limited, *New Delhi*
Prentice-Hall of Japan, Inc., *Tokyo*
Simon & Schuster Asia Pte. Ltd., *Singapore*
Editora Prentice-Hall do Brasil, Ltda., *Rio de Janeiro*

Contents

Introduction

This book provides instruction and practice in reading globes and various types of maps. It introduces concepts in geography a person needs to interpret globes and maps. The many colorful globes and maps in this book are the kind adults encounter both in daily living and on such tests as the GED.

The format of the chapters in this book is consistent throughout. Each chapter carefully integrates reading, writing, and thinking skills. Chapters begin with **How Much Do You Already Know?**—four brief multiple-choice questions that serve as a preview of the chapter's content. The instruction covers concepts in a step-by-step manner. Short-answer questions throughout the instruction allow students to apply concepts immediately. **How Carefully Did You Read?**—an end-of-chapter exercise made up of both multiple-choice and short-answer questions—allows students to review and apply all the concepts covered in a chapter.

How Much Do You Already Know?

Choose the correct completion for each statement. If you are not sure about an answer, do not guess.

1. The most accurate model of the earth is a

   ☐ a. flat map.
   ☐ b. globe.
   ☐ c. celestial map.

2. A country can be shown in the greatest detail by a

   ☐ a. flat map.
   ☐ b. globe.
   ☐ c. celestial map.

3. An advantage that a globe has over a flat map is that a globe

   ☐ a. shows the size, shape, and location of land and water areas accurately.
   ☐ b. shows more information.
   ☐ c. is always easier to use.

4. An advantage that a flat map has over a globe is that a flat map

   ☐ a. pictures the entire earth.
   ☐ b. shows directions and distances between places accurately.
   ☐ c. can be folded up and carried around.

Check your answers on page 135.

Globes and Maps

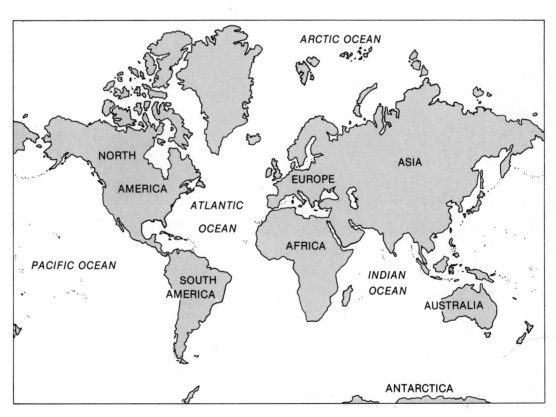

Globes and maps are representations, or likenesses, of the earth. A **globe** pictures the entire earth—all its land and water areas. A **map,** on the other hand, may show the entire earth, but most often pictures only a part of it. For example, a map may show only one country, one city, or one town—or perhaps only a single neighborhood.

Globes and maps have other important differences, too. The most obvious one is that a globe is a sphere. It is round, just as the earth, itself, is nearly round. A map is a drawing of all or part of the earth on a flat surface.

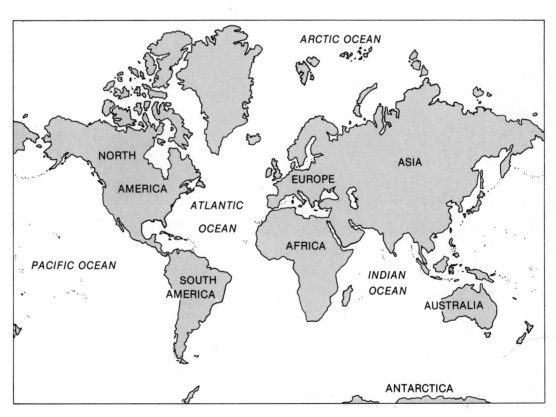

Figure 1.1 A Flat Map of the World

ACCURACY AND DISTORTION

Because a globe is a sphere, it shows the size, shape, and location of land and water areas on the earth accurately. This is not true of a flat map, where the size, shape, or location of land and water areas is distorted—that is, inaccurately pictured.

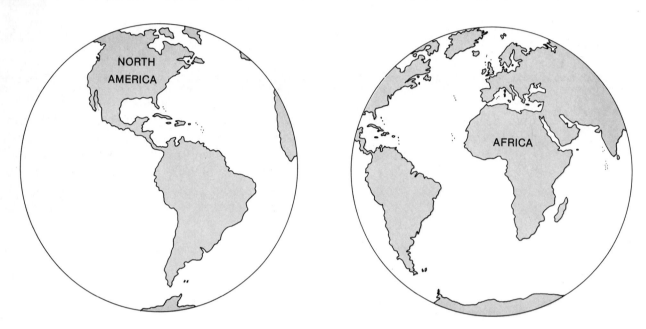

Figure 1.2 The Earth's Surface As Shown on a Globe

Compare Figure 1.1 on page 3 and Figure 1.2, above. Figure 1.1 shows a flat map of the world. Figure 1.2 shows the earth's surface as it appears on a globe.

 Find North America and Africa on the flat map. They are two of the world's

seven **continents,** or large land areas. Compare their sizes on the flat map.

Which appears to be larger? _____

Find the same two continents on the globe. Now which of them appears to be

larger? _____

On the flat map, North America seems larger than Africa. However, the globe, which is a true likeness of the earth, shows that Africa is much larger than North America (actually, by more than 2 million square miles).

The shapes of land areas on the flat map are accurate, but their sizes are not. Why is this so? Imagine for a moment a grapefruit with the earth's land and water areas drawn on it. Think of peeling the skin off the grapefruit in one piece. Figure 1.3 shows what the peel might look like.

The peel is not in the shape of a rectangle, the way many flat maps are. Imagine stretching parts of the peel so that it takes on the shape of a rectangular flat map. What would happen to the drawings of the land and water areas? The stretching would change their sizes or shapes.

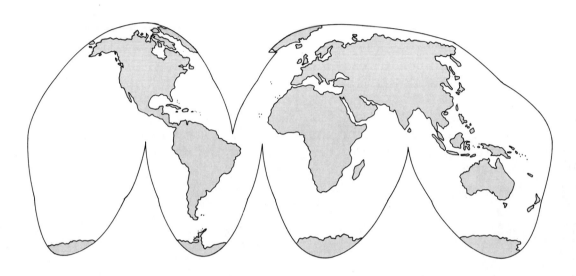

Figure 1.3 The Earth's Land and Water Areas Drawn on a Grapefruit Peel

In a sense, a flat map is drawn as though a globe were peeled and stretched like the grapefruit. Therefore, sizes and shapes of land and water areas on it are distorted.

 Study the illustration of the peeled grapefruit (Figure 1.3). Making a flat map of the peel would cause more stretching in some areas than in others. Where would the land and water areas be most distorted on the map—at the top and bottom, or in the middle? _____

The greatest amount of stretching, and therefore distortion, would occur at the top and bottom. That is why North America looks larger than Africa on the flat map.

ADVANTAGES AND DISADVANTAGES

Even though flat maps are not as accurate as globes, they do have certain advantages.

Can you think of two advantages that flat maps have over globes?

1. _____

2. _____

One important advantage is that flat maps are easier to use. They can be folded and carried wherever you go. A second advantage is that flat maps show much more detail than globes. Globes, as you have seen, always picture *all* of the earth. It would take a huge globe, then, to show details like ponds, roads, and small towns—things that many flat maps include. Obviously, a globe that would be big enough to show such details would be awkward, if not impossible, to use.

Of course, globes are useful objects, too. For example, because a globe is a true likeness of the earth, not only are all sizes and shapes accurate. Distances and directions between places are accurate as well. That is why ship captains and airline pilots plot their trips on a globe rather than on a flat map.

DID YOU KNOW that the oldest known maps are over 4,000 years old? These are land surveys carved on clay tablets by Babylonian people about 2300 B.C. These crude maps show settlements, streams, hills, and mountains in what is now northern Iraq.

How Carefully Did You Read?

A. Choose the correct completion for each statement.

1. A globe is a likeness of

   ☐ a. part of the earth.
   ☐ b. all of the earth.
   ☐ c. land areas on the earth.

2. A globe is more accurate than a flat map because a globe

   ☐ a. shows more detail.
   ☐ b. is shaped almost like the earth.
   ☐ c. contains more information.

3. The differences between globes and maps are

   ☐ a. impossible to see.
   ☐ b. not very important.
   ☐ c. quite important.

4. Compared to a globe, a flat map

   ☐ a. is easier to use.
   ☐ b. shows less information.
   ☐ c. shows shapes more accurately.

B. Label the seven continents and the four oceans indicated on the map in Figure 1.4.

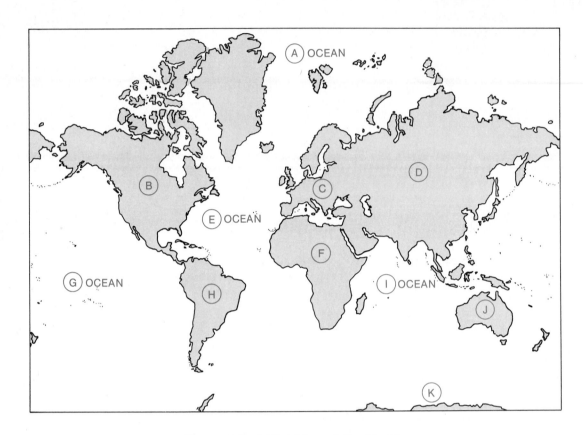

Figure 1.4   A Flat Map of the World

A. _____

B. _____

C. _____

D. _____

E. _____

F. _____

G. _____

H. _____

I. _____

J. _____

K. _____

Check your answers on page 135.

Look back at **How Much Do You Already Know?** on page 2. Did you complete each statement correctly? If not, can you do so now?

DID YOU KNOW that 200 years ago in England, globes were so popular that many people carried small globes or wore them as jewelry? These tiny globes were often kept inside leather cases that had a celestial map (a map of the heavens) drawn on the inner surface.

How Much Do You Already Know?

Choose the correct completion for each statement. If you are not sure about an answer, do not guess.

1. Since a globe is a sphere, you can see

   ☐ a. only about half the earth at a time.

   ☐ b. the entire earth at once.

   ☐ c. only a small part of the earth at a time.

2. The equator is

   ☐ a. a country in South America.

   ☐ b. an imaginary line around the middle of the earth.

   ☐ c. a line that divides North America from South America.

3. The point at the very bottom of a globe is called the

   ☐ a. North Pole.

   ☐ b. Arctic Circle.

   ☐ c. South Pole.

4. North America is in the

   ☐ a. Western Hemisphere.

   ☐ b. Southern Hemisphere.

   ☐ c. Eastern Hemisphere.

Check your answers on page 135.

Features of a Globe

2

As you learned in Chapter 1, a globe is a model of the entire earth. Because the earth is nearly round, a globe, which is a sphere, is the truest model of the earth. That means the size, shape, and location of land and water areas on a globe are pictured correctly. So, too, are distances between places on a globe.

THE POLES AND THE EQUATOR

The circle in Figure 2.1 represents one view of a globe. The figure shows three important features of a globe. The point at the very top of the globe represents the **North Pole.** The point at a very bottom of the globe represents the **South Pole.** There is a line halfway between the North Pole and the South Pole. It represents the **equator** [ih KWAY ter], an imaginary line around the middle of the earth that separates the northern half of the world from the southern half.

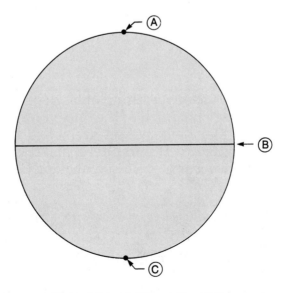

Figure 2.1   A View of a Globe

In Figure 2.1, arrows point to these three important parts of the globe. Tell which part of the globe each arrow points to.

Arrow **A** points to the _____ .

Arrow **B** points to the _____ .

Arrow **C** points to the _____ .

The North Pole is indicated by Arrow **A**; the equator, by Arrow **B**; and the South Pole, by Arrow **C**.

DID YOU KNOW that in 1492, the same year Columbus first sailed to America, a man named Martin Behaim, of Nuremberg, Germany, made a globe 20 inches in diameter? His globe is believed to be the oldest in existence.

THE HEMISPHERES

Since it is a sphere, you cannot see everything on a globe at once. Figures 2.2 through 2.5 show four different views of a globe. Each of the four views shows a major **hemisphere** [HEM us fear] of the earth. The four hemispheres are called the **Northern Hemisphere,** the **Southern Hemisphere,** the **Eastern Hemisphere,** and the **Western Hemisphere.** (The word *hemisphere* is made up of two words from the ancient Greeks: *hemi* means *half,* and *sphere* means *ball.*)

 If you look straight down on a globe from the North Pole, you will be looking at the Northern Hemisphere. This hemisphere includes all the land and water areas north of the equator. Which figure on page 13 shows the Northern Hemisphere? _____

Figure 2.2

Figure 2.3

Figure 2.4

Figure 2.5

If your vantage point is looking at the globe from the South Pole, you will see the Southern Hemisphere. This hemisphere includes all the land and water areas south of the equator. Which figure on page 13 shows the Southern Hemisphere?

_____

While geographers have never agreed on an exact line dividing the Eastern and Western Hemispheres, they accept that the Eastern Hemisphere includes the continents of Africa, Asia, Australia, and Europe and the water and small land areas around them. Which figure on page 13 shows the Eastern Hemisphere?

_____

Geographers also agree that the Western Hemisphere consists of the North and South American continents and the water and small land areas around them. Which figure on page 13 shows the Western Hemisphere? _____

If you look closely at the illustrations, you will see that each continent is really in two hemispheres. For example, Australia is in both the Southern and Eastern Hemispheres. Which continent do you live on? _____ Which hemispheres is your continent in? _____ and _____

    The Northern Hemisphere is shown in Figure 2.2; the Southern, in 2.3; the Eastern, in 2.4; and the Western in 2.5. If you live in North America, for example, you live in both the Northern and Western Hemispheres.

DID YOU KNOW that Duke Frederick of Holstein-Gottorp had an 11-foot globe made in 1664? The Duke's globe showed the world on the outside and the heavens on the inside. A door let as many as twelve people at a time into the globe.

How Carefully Did You Read?

A. Choose the correct completion for each statement.

1. The word *hemisphere* is a word for

   ☐ a. a pole.
   ☐ b. half the earth's surface.
   ☐ c. a globe.

2. The equator

   ☐ a. is a hemisphere.
   ☐ b. divides north from south.
   ☐ c. separates continents from each other.

3. The land and water areas above the equator are in the

   ☐ a. Southern Hemisphere.
   ☐ b. Eastern Hemisphere.
   ☐ c. Northern Hemisphere.

4. The Eastern Hemisphere includes all of

   ☐ a. Africa.
   ☐ b. South America.
   ☐ c. Antarctica.

5. One continent in the Western Hemisphere is

☐ a. South America.
☐ b. Europe.
☐ c. Asia.

6. The point at the very top of the globe is called the

☐ a. North Pole.
☐ b. South Pole.
☐ c. equator.

B. Use Figures 2.2 through 2.5 on page 13 to answer the following.

1. The name for all land and water areas below the equator is the _____
   Hemisphere.

2. The name for all land and water areas above the equator is the _____
   Hemisphere.

3. The largest of the seven continents appears to be _____ .

4. The second largest continent appears to be _____ .

5. Are most of earth's land areas north or south of the equator? _____

6. The continent of Europe is in both the _____ and the _____
   Hemispheres.

7. The Western Hemisphere includes the continents of _____ and

   _____ .

8. The two continents that the equator passes through are _____ and

   _____ .

Check your answers on page 135.

Look back at **How Much Do You Already Know?** on page 10. Did you complete each statement correctly? If not, can you do so now?

DID YOU KNOW that one of the smallest countries in South America takes its name from the Spanish word for *equator*? That country, named Ecuador, lies on the west coast of the continent, between Colombia and Peru.

How Much Do You Already Know?

Choose the correct completion for each statement. If you are not sure about an answer, do not guess.

1. The prime meridian is

   ☐ a. an imaginary line on the earth.

   ☐ b. the same as the equator.

   ☐ c. a direction on a globe.

2. North and south directions are measured from the

   ☐ a. equator.

   ☐ b. South Pole.

   ☐ c. North Pole.

3. An example of a cardinal direction is

   ☐ a. SW.

   ☐ b. NE.

   ☐ c. W.

4. An example of an intermediate direction is

   ☐ a. south.

   ☐ b. northwest.

   ☐ c. east.

Check your answers on page 135.

Directions on a Globe

3

NORTH AND SOUTH DIRECTIONS

You already know from Chapter 2 that the equator is an imaginary line that circles the middle of the earth. All north and south directions are measured from the equator.

Figure 3.1   Directions North and South of the Equator

Look at Figure 3.1. What is the name of the continent that is above, or north of, the equator? _____

What is the name of the lower continent that the equator passes through in Figure 3.1? _____

Figure 3.1 shows that the continent of North America is above, or north of, the equator. The equator passes through the continent of South America, which is mostly below, or south of, the equator.

EAST AND WEST DIRECTIONS

A second important imaginary line on the earth is known as the **prime meridian** [muh RID ee an]. It goes halfway around the earth. As Figure 3.2 shows, the prime meridian runs from the North Pole through the town of Greenwich, England, to the South Pole. All east and west directions are measured from the prime meridian. (The term *prime meridian* comes from two Latin words. *Prime* means *first. Meridian* means *midday,* the moment when the sun reaches its highest point in the sky.)

Figure 3.2   Directions East and West of the Prime Meridian

 Look at Figure 3.2. Do you recognize the large continent that the prime meridian passes through? What is its name? _____

What is the name of the lower continent to the west of the prime meridian in

Figure 3.2? _____

The large continent that the prime meridian passes through is Africa. The lower continent to the west of the prime meridian is South America.

CARDINAL DIRECTIONS

The directions north, south, east, and west are known as the **cardinal directions,** or principal directions. Cardinal directions are usually written as **N, S, E,** and **W.** Figure 3.3 shows the cardinal directions.

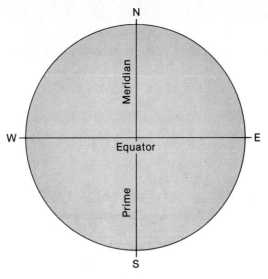

Figure 3.3 The Cardinal Directions

 Imagine that you are facing north. Which direction would be on your right?

_____

Imagine you are facing south. Now which direction would be on your right?

_____ Which direction would be behind you? _____

When you face north, east is on your right. When you face south, west is on your right and north is behind you.

INTERMEDIATE DIRECTIONS

Not every direction on a globe is a cardinal direction. Other directions are called **intermediate directions,** directions *between* the cardinal directions. Intermediate directions are often used in telling the direction between two locations on a globe.

Figure 3.2 on page 20 shows that the continent of Asia is both north and east of Africa. In other words, its direction from Africa is northeast—that is, partway between the cardinal directions north and east.

 Figure 3.2 shows that the continent of South America is which direction from

the continent of Europe? _____

Figure 3.2 shows that South America is south and west of Europe. Therefore, it is southwest of Europe.

Directions are measured *from,* or *in relation to,* the starting point. When you measure the direction that South America is *from* Europe, Europe is the starting point.

 If you measure the direction from South America to Europe, which continent

is the starting point? _____

Which direction is Europe from South America? _____

Directions on a Globe 21

When you measure the direction that Europe is from South America, South America is the starting point. Europe is northeast of the starting point, South America.

You already know that the four cardinal directions are N, S, E, and W. You also know that northeast and southwest are intermediate directions.

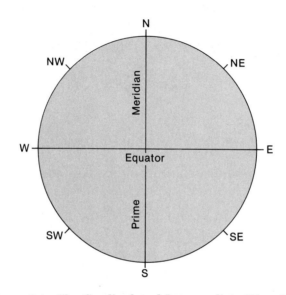 Besides these, there are two more intermediate directions. Can you figure out

what they are? _____ and _____

If you said southeast and northwest, you are right. Southeast is partway between south and east. Northwest is partway between north and west.

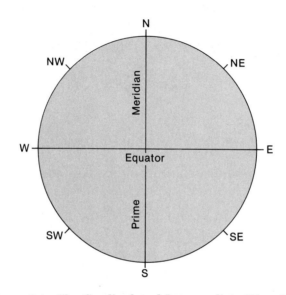

Figure 3.4   The Cardinal and Intermediate Directions

Figure 3.4 shows both the cardinal and intermediate directions. The intermediate directions are usually written **NE, SE, SW,** and **NW.**

How Carefully Did You Read?

A. Choose the correct completion for each statement.

1. East and west directions are measured from the

   ☐ a. equator.
   ☐ b. prime meridian.
   ☐ c. poles.

2. The prime meridian runs

   ☐ a. alongside the equator.
   ☐ b. through Greenwich, England.
   ☐ c. through North America.

3. Whenever you face east, the direction on your right is

   ☐ a. north.
   ☐ b. south.
   ☐ c. west.

4. The letters **N, S, E,** and **W** represent

   ☐ a. cardinal directions.
   ☐ b. points on a globe.
   ☐ c. intermediate directions.

5. Intermediate directions are the directions

☐ a. along the equator.
☐ b. on the prime meridian.
☐ c. partway between the cardinal directions.

6. Asia is northeast of South America, so South America is

☐ a. northeast of Asia.
☐ b. southeast of Asia.
☐ c. southwest of Asia.

B. What you have read about cardinal and intermediate directions on a globe also applies to maps. Use the map of part of the United States in Figure 3.5 to answer the following.

Figure 3.5   The Southeastern United States

Note: This figure W—|—E with the map shows that north is at the top of the map.

1. The map shows all or parts of how many states? _____

2. The state farthest to the southeast is _____ .

3. The state that reaches farthest to the east is _____ .

4. The state in the extreme northwest corner of the map is _____ .

5. North Carolina is bordered by the state of _____ on the north.

6. The two states that border on Mississippi on the west are _____

   and _____ .

7. The two states that form the northern border of Florida are _____

   and _____ .

8. In Alabama, to go from Tuscaloosa to Montgomery, the direction you would travel

   is _____ .

9. In Georgia, the direction from Albany to Savannah is _____ .

10. Little Rock, Arkansas, lies _____ of Fort Smith, Arkansas.

11. Fort Smith, Arkansas, lies _____ of Little Rock, Arkansas.

Check your answers on page 135.

Look back at **How Much Do You Already Know?** on page 18. Did you complete each statement correctly? If not, can you do so now?

DID YOU KNOW that the idea of one prime meridian has been in use only since 1884? Until then, countries often established their own. For example, France's ran through Paris; Italy's, through Rome; and the United States', through Washington, D.C. Without a single starting place for telling east and west directions, there was always the possibility of confusion when the locations of places were communicated. Finally, most countries accepted the prime meridian shown on English charts, which were used by sailors of many nations.

How Much Do You Already Know?

Choose the correct completion for each statement. If you are not sure about an answer, do not guess.

1. Lines that run east-west on a globe are known as

   ☐ a. latitude lines.
   ☐ b. meridians.
   ☐ c. longitude lines.

2. Lines that run north-south on a globe are known as

   ☐ a. latitude lines.
   ☐ b. parallels.
   ☐ c. longitude lines.

3. The lines that run east-west on a globe

   ☐ a. meet at the poles.
   ☐ b. never meet.
   ☐ c. meet at the prime meridian.

4. Distances on a globe are measured in

   ☐ a. feet.
   ☐ b. miles.
   ☐ c. degrees.

Check your answers on page 135.

Locating Places on a Globe

4

 To locate places on a globe, you need to use east-west and north-south lines. You are already familiar with two of these.

 What is the name of the imaginary line that runs east-west around the middle of the earth? _____

Another imaginary line runs halfway around the world—from the North Pole through Greenwich, England, to the South Pole. What is its name?

_____

The equator runs east-west all the way around the middle of the earth. The prime meridian runs halfway around the earth from the north pole to the south pole.

The location of a particular place on a globe is the point where a north-south line intersects with, or crosses, an east-west line. For example, Figure 4.1 shows where the prime meridian crosses the equator. That point is a particular place on a globe. It is the only place that can be accurately located in Figure 4.1 because it is the only point where two lines intersect.

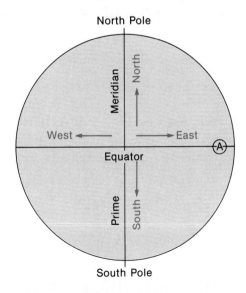

Figure 4.1 The Intersection of the Equator and the Prime Meridian

Suppose you wanted to describe the location of the place marked **A** in Figure 4.1. You could say only that point **A** lies on the equator somewhere east of the prime meridian. But since the equator is about 25,000 miles long, that is not a very accurate description. (Imagine telling friends that you live on Oak Street, when that street might be several miles long. It would not be easy for them to find you.)

Since places are found all over the globe, what is needed are more north-south and east-west lines to find locations. Fortunately, globes have these lines.

LATITUDE AND LONGITUDE LINES

The lines that run east-west in Figure 4.2 are **latitude lines** or **parallels.** Latitude lines are also called parallels because any two of them are always the same distance apart all the way around the world. Latitude lines are used to measure distances north or south of the equator.

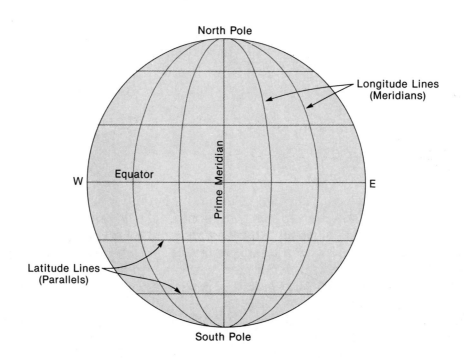

Figure 4.2   Latitude Lines and Longitude Lines on a Globe

The lines that run north-south in Figure 4.2 are **longitude lines** [LON jih tood], or **meridians.** Longitude lines are used to measure distances east or west of the prime meridian. As the figure shows, longitude lines are not always the same distance apart.

 At what two places do longitude lines meet? _____

Where are longitude lines farthest apart from each other? _____

Longitude lines meet at the North and South Poles. They are farthest apart at the equator.

MEASURING WITH LATITUDE LINES

Now look at Figure 4.3. Latitude lines on a globe (and longitude lines, too, for that matter) are measured in degrees. Why degrees? A globe is round, like a circle. Circles are measured in degrees, so measurements on a globe are given in degrees.

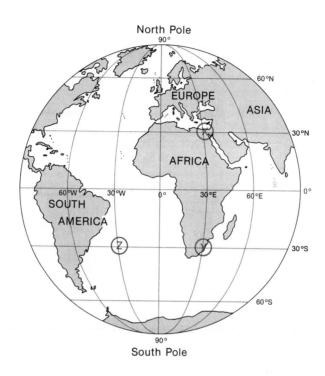

Figure 4.3   Degrees of Latitude and Longitude on a Globe

As the figure shows, the starting point for measuring latitude lines is the equator. The equator is at zero degrees, which is usually written 0°. All other latitude lines are said to be a certain number of degrees north or south of the equator, ending at the poles.

Because a circle has 360°, the distance around the whole globe is 360°. From the equator to the North Pole is one-quarter the way around the globe, or 90°. Therefore, between the equator and the North Pole, there are 90 degrees of latitude. That means there could be 90 latitude lines north of the equator. (There could also be 90 lines south of the equator.) Obviously, so many lines would clutter a globe and make it very hard to read. Therefore, only some latitude lines are shown.

How many degrees are there between latitude lines in Figure 4.3? _____

Latitude lines in Figure 4.3 are drawn at 30-degree intervals.
With latitude lines, it is possible to tell where a point is in relation to the equator.

For example, look at point **X** in Figure 4.3. Is point **X** north or south of the

equator? _____

How many degrees from the equator is point **X**? _____

Point **X**, the figure shows, is 60 degrees north of the equator. This is usually written **60°N.**

 Now find point **Y** in Figure 4.3. How many degrees north or south is point **Y** from the equator? _____

Point **Y** is 30°S, or 30 degrees south, of the equator.

MEASURING WITH LONGITUDE LINES

Longitude lines, or meridians, you will remember, are used to show distances east or west of the prime meridian. Since the prime meridian is the starting point, it is at zero degrees longitude, or 0°. Opposite the prime meridian is the 180° longitude line, halfway around the world. All longitude lines between 0° and 180° are said to be a certain number of degrees east or west of the prime meridian.

 Point **X** in Figure 4.3, you learned, is 60 degrees north (60°N) of the equator. *typo*

It also lies on a meridian, or longitude line. Is point **X** east or west of the prime

meridian? _____

How many degrees from the prime meridian is point **X**? _____

 Point **X** is east of the prime meridian by 30 degrees (30°). It is at 30°E.

Now find point **Y** in Figure 4.3. How many degrees east or west is this point

from the prime meridian? _____

Point **Y** is 30°E of the prime meridian.

LOCATING PLACES BY LATITUDE AND LONGITUDE

Now that you know the latitude and longitude of point **X**, you can give an accurate location of the place. Its location is written like this: **60°N 30°E.**

When a location is written, the latitude is always given first, followed by the longitude. Since all latitudes are either north or south, the letter **N** or **S** signals a latitude. Because longitudes are either east or west, the letter **E** or **W** signals a longitude. The words *latitude* and *longitude* are not written.

 What is the location, in degrees of latitude and longitude, of point **Y** in Figure

4.3? _____

Find point **Z** in Figure 4.3. What is its location, in degrees of latitude and

longitude? _____

Point **Y** is at 30°S 30°E. Point **Z** is at 30°S 30°W.

How Carefully Did You Read?

A. Choose the correct completion for each statement.

1. Latitude lines on a globe show

   ☐ a. the locations of places.
   ☐ b. distances east or west of the prime meridian.
   ☐ c. distances north or south of the equator.

2. Longitude lines on a globe show

   ☐ a. the locations of places.
   ☐ b. distances east or west of the prime meridian.
   ☐ c. distances north or south of the equator.

3. Latitude lines are also called parallels because they

   ☐ a. never meet.
   ☐ b. meet at the North Pole.
   ☐ c. meet at the equator.

4. *Meridians* is another name for

   ☐ a. parallels.
   ☐ b. latitude lines.
   ☐ c. longitude lines.

5. The distance all the way around a globe is

☐ a. 90 degrees.
☐ b. 180 degrees.
☐ c. 360 degrees.

6. The expression **60°W** indicates

☐ a. a longitude line.
☐ b. a latitude line.
☐ c. the prime meridian.

7. In Figure 4.3 on page 29, the place at 30°S 60°W is in

☐ a. Europe.
☐ b. Africa.
☐ c. South America.

B. Figure 4.4 shows the whole surface of a globe as though it were stretched out. Refer to it to complete the following statements.

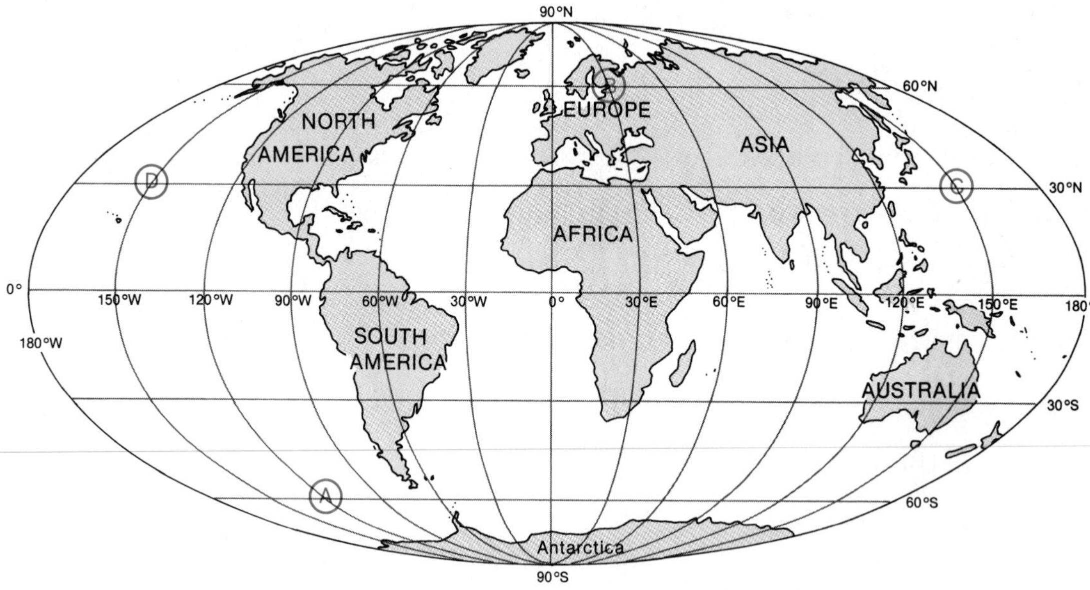

Figure 4.4 Degrees of Latitude and Longitude on a "Stretched" Globe

1. The latitude line that goes through the continent of Australia is labeled _____ .

2. The expression **90°N** indicates the location of the _____ .

3. The longitude line that passes through the middle of the continent of South America

   is labeled _____ .

4. The southernmost part of the continent of Africa lies between these two latitude lines:

_____ and _____ .

5. Point **B** is located at _____ .

6. 30°N 150°E indicates the location of point _____ .

7. 30°N 150°W is the location of point _____ .

8. Point **A** is located at _____ .

Check your answers on page 135.

Look back at **How Much Do You Already Know?** on page 26. Did you complete each statement correctly? If not, can you do so now?

DID YOU KNOW that the exact distance around the world at the equator is 24,901.55 miles? When Columbus set sail on his first voyage, however, he thought the distance was only 18,000 miles. That is why he thought he had reached the East Indies when, in fact, he had sailed only as far as the Americas.

How Much Do You Already Know?

Choose the correct completion for each statement. If you are not sure about an answer, do not guess.

1. When it is 2:00 P.M. in Boston, Massachusetts, in San Francisco, California, it is

    ☐ a. earlier.
    ☐ b. 2:00 P.M.
    ☐ c. later.

2. In the United States, the time in two towns is different when the towns are in

    ☐ a. the same time zone.
    ☐ b. different states.
    ☐ c. different time zones.

3. Time around the world is measured from the

    ☐ a. equator.
    ☐ b. North and South Poles.
    ☐ c. prime meridian.

4. The world has

    ☐ a. 15 time zones.
    ☐ b. 24 time zones.
    ☐ c. 360 time zones.

Check your answers on page 136.

Longitude and Time Zones

5

TIME ZONES IN THE UNITED STATES

If you watch television, you already know that it is not the same time everywhere at once. For example, suppose you live in Boston, Massachusetts. At 4:00 P.M. you turn on your TV set to watch the start of a football game in Los Angeles, California. The time in that West Coast city is 1:00 P.M. Viewers in Chicago, Illinois, who want to watch the start of the game will turn on their TV sets at 3:00 P.M. To anyone watching in Denver, Colorado, the time will be 2:00 P.M. Each city is in a different **time zone**, as shown in Figure 5.1.

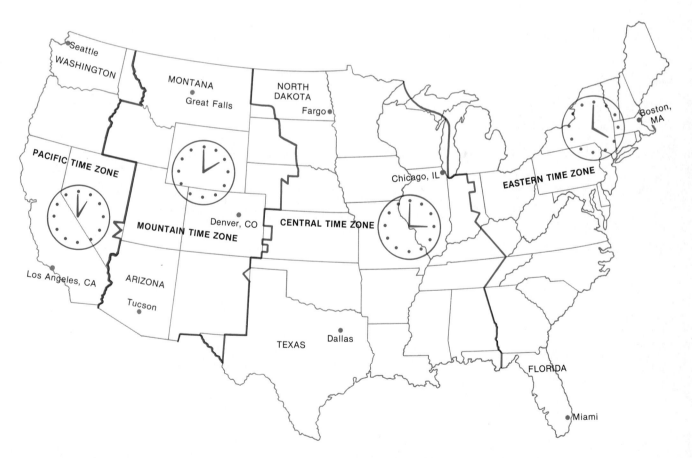

Figure 5.1 Time Zones in the Continental United States

Figure 5.1 shows that the forty-eight states that border on each other are spread through four time zones. (Alaska and Hawaii are in two other time zones.) The heavy lines in the figure mark the borders of the four time zones. Can you guess why the borders are not straight lines?

The time zone borders zig-zag as a convenience to people living near them. If borders didn't zig-zag, they might run through towns. Think how confusing it would be to live in a town split by two time zones. If it were 8:00 A.M. on the east side of town, it would be 7:00 A.M. on the west side!

 Figure 5.1 shows that Los Angeles lies in the Pacific Time Zone. In which time zone is each of these cities?

Boston _____

Chicago _____

Denver _____

Boston is in the Eastern Time Zone; Chicago, Central; Denver, Mountain.

TIME WITHIN A TIME ZONE

Figure 5.1 shows that when it is 1:00 P.M. in Los Angeles, it is also 1:00 P.M. throughout the entire Pacific Time Zone. Even though Seattle, Washington, is nearly 1,000 miles north of Los Angeles, it is on the same time as Los Angeles. Similarly, when it is 2:00 P.M. in Denver, it is also 2:00 P.M. in Great Falls, Montana, and in Tucson, Arizona. The time of day is always the same in all the places within any time zone.

When it is 3:00 P.M. in Chicago, what time is it in Fargo, North Dakota, and

in Dallas, Texas? _____

When it is 4:00 P.M. in Boston, what time is it in Miami, Florida? _____

Why is the time in Denver different from that in Boston? _____

When it is 3:00 P.M. in Chicago, it is also 3:00 P.M. in Fargo and in Dallas. Likewise, when it is 4:00 P.M. in Boston, it is 4:00 P.M. in Miami. The times in Denver and Boston are different because they are not in the same time zone.

If you live in one of the forty-eight states shown on the map in Figure 5.1, you can find the time zone you live in. Find your state. Locate the position of your town or city within the state. What time zone are you in?

TIME ZONES AROUND THE WORLD

The earth, you may already know, is not motionless. It spins from west to east on its axis, which is an imaginary line that runs through the center of the earth. (See Figure 5.2.) It takes twenty-four hours, or one day, for the earth to make one complete spin, or rotation, on its axis.

Each point on the earth faces the sun directly only once each day. At that time, the sun seems to be overhead. It is then noon, or midday, at that point on the earth.

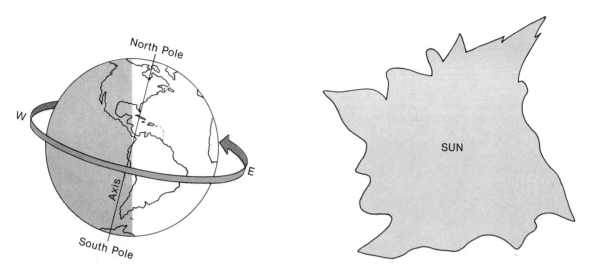

Figure 5.2 The Earth Rotating on Its Axis

When Greenwich, England, faces the sun each day, it is then noon there. Greenwich sits on the prime meridian, so when Greenwich faces the sun, the whole prime meridian faces the sun.

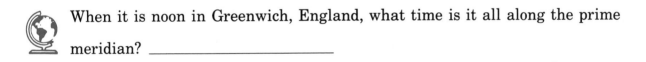

When it is noon in Greenwich, England, what time is it all along the prime meridian? _____

When it is noon in Greenwich, it is noon at every point on the prime meridian, from the North Pole to the South Pole.

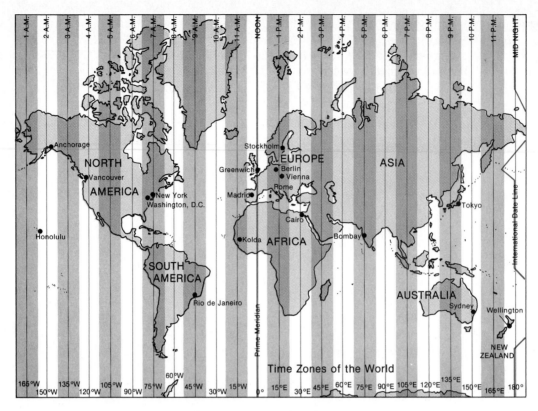

Figure 5.3   World Time Zones

Figure 5.3 shows all the time zones in the world. Find the prime meridian near the center of the figure.

 What is the time at the prime meridian in Figure 5.3? _____

Notice that the prime meridian is in the center of a time zone. What is the time

throughout that time zone? _____

In Figure 5.3, the time at the prime meridian is noon. It is noon throughout the time zone. (Remember that it is always the same time at every point within a time zone.)
Time around the world is measured from the prime meridian. Figure 5.3 shows what time it is at any place in the world when it is noon in Greenwich.

 Using Figure 5.3, count how many time zones there are in the world. How many

does the figure show? _____

There are twenty-four time zones in the world, one to contain, in a sense, each hour of a day.
Notice in Figure 5.3 that there is a meridian, or longitude line, right in the middle of each time zone. The meridians are evenly spaced.

 How many degrees are there between the meridians in Figure 5.3? _____

There are 15 degrees, or 15°, between meridians. That means that each time zone is 15° across. Why are time zones 15° across, not more and not less?

As noted, there are twenty-four time zones. The distance around the globe, as you read in Chapter 4, is 360°. If you divide twenty-four time zones into 360°, you find that each time zone must be 15° across. (Another way to think of this is that the earth rotates 15° on its axis each hour.)

Take a closer look at Figure 5.3 to see how times around the world are measured from the time at the prime meridian.

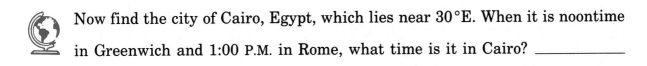 Find the city of Rome, Italy. Rome is east of the prime meridian. What meridian, or longitude line, does Rome lie nearest to? _____

When it is noontime on the prime meridian, what time is it in Rome?

_____

Rome is closest to the meridian at 15°E. It is in the time zone that is just to the east of the zone with the prime meridian. Therefore, it is one hour later in Rome than on the prime meridian, or 1:00 P.M.

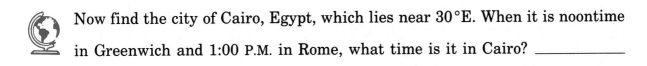 Now find the city of Cairo, Egypt, which lies near 30°E. When it is noontime in Greenwich and 1:00 P.M. in Rome, what time is it in Cairo? _____

The time in Cairo—2:00 P.M.—is two hours *ahead of,* or later than, the time on the prime meridian (and one hour ahead of the time in Rome). This shows that when you travel east, the time becomes one hour later as you pass into each new time zone.

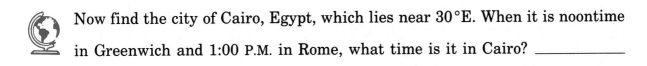 Find the town of Kolda, which is in Africa. Kolda lies near 15 degrees west longitude (15°W). What is the time in Kolda when it is noontime on the prime

meridian? _____

Now look for Rio de Janeiro in South America. It lies near 45°W. When it is

noontime in Greenwich, what time is it in Rio? _____

The time in Kolda is 11:00 A.M., one hour *behind,* or earlier than, the time on the prime meridian. In Rio it is 9:00 A.M., or three hours behind Greenwich. This shows that when you travel west, the time becomes one hour earlier as you pass into each new time zone.

Find longitude 180° in Figure 5.3. It is the point where east meets west. What is its special name? _____

What time is it at longitude 180° when it is noontime on the prime meridian?

_____

The special name for the meridian at 180° is the **International Date Line.** It is midnight there when it is noon on the prime meridian.

DID YOU KNOW that daylight saving time was first used in Germany in 1915, during World War I? Clocks were set ahead one hour to make more use of daylight hours and to save energy. The United States first went on daylight saving time on March 30, 1918.

How Carefully Did You Read?

A. Choose the correct completion for each statement. You may want to refer to the figures in this chapter for help in completing some statements.

1. When the time is 10:00 A.M. in Los Angeles, on the west coast of the United States, the time in New York City, on the east coast, is

   ☐ a. 7:00 A.M.

   ☐ b. 10:00 A.M.

   ☐ c. 1:00 P.M.

2. There is a one-hour time difference for every

   ☐ a. 15° of longitude.

   ☐ b. 24° of longitude.

   ☐ c. 180° of longitude.

3. When you travel east into the next time zone, the time

   ☐ a. is one hour earlier.

   ☐ b. is one hour later.

   ☐ c. stays the same.

4. When the time is 3:00 P.M. in the Central Time Zone of the United States, the time in the Mountain Time Zone is

   ☐ a. 4:00 P.M.

   ☐ b. 3:00 P.M.

   ☐ c. 2:00 P.M.

5. 180° longitude marks the location of the

☐ a. International Date Line.

☐ b. equator.

☐ c. prime meridian.

6. Compared to the time at the prime meridian, the time at 30°W is always

☐ a. the same.

☐ b. later.

☐ c. earlier.

7. When it is noon on the prime meridian, on the International Date Line it is

☐ a. also noon.

☐ b. 6:00 P.M.

☐ c. midnight.

B. Use Figure 5.3 on page 38 to complete these statements.

1. The figure shows the time in Stockholm, Sweden, to be _____ .

2. When the time is 4:00 A.M. at 120°W, the time at 120°E is _____ .

3. When the time is 7:00 A.M. in New York City, the time in Washington, D.C., is

   _____ .

4. If it is noon in Madrid, Spain, the time in any city in South America is sure to be

   _____ than noon.

5. When the time is 1:00 P.M. in Berlin, Germany, the time in Vienna, Austria, is

   _____ .

6. When the time is 5:00 P.M. at 75°E, the time at 135°W is _____ .

7. The figure shows the time in Anchorage, Alaska, to be _____ .

8. If it is 4:00 A.M. in Vancouver, B.C., Canada, the time in any city on Canada's east

   coast is sure to be _____ than 4:00 A.M.

9. Between Bombay, India, and Sydney, Australia, there is a time difference of

_____ hours.

10. If it is 1:00 A.M. in Honolulu, Hawaii, in Wellington, New Zealand, it is _____ .

Check your answers on page 136.

Look back at **How Much Do You Already Know?** on page 34. Did you complete each statement correctly? If not, can you do so now?

DID YOU KNOW that the railroads were responsible for establishing the four time zones—Pacific, Mountain, Central, and Eastern—in the continental United States? Railroad time zones began on October 11, 1883. Congress later passed the Standard Time Act on March 19, 1918. Before the time zones were established, most people set their watches when the sun was overhead, guessing that it was then noon. That caused a lot of confusion. In Michigan there were twenty-seven different local times used around the state. There were thirty-eight in Wisconsin, twenty-seven in Illinois, and twenty-three in Indiana.

How Much Do You Already Know?

Choose the correct completion for each statement. If you are not sure about an answer, do not guess.

1. Compared to the object it represents, a scale model is

   ☐ a. smaller.
   ☐ b. shaped differently.
   ☐ c. smaller and shaped differently.

2. When a model's scale is 1 inch to the foot, 1 inch on the model represents

   ☐ a. 1 foot on the real object.
   ☐ b. 1 inch on the real object.
   ☐ c. 1 foot plus 1 inch on the real object.

3. Measurements on a globe are usually given in

   ☐ a. inches.
   ☐ b. feet.
   ☐ c. degrees.

4. A degree measured in miles along the equator, compared to one measured along the parallel at 40°N, is

   ☐ a. longer.
   ☐ b. the same length.
   ☐ c. shorter.

Check your answers on page 136.

Finding Distances on a Globe

6

MODELS AND SCALES

 A globe is a model of the earth—not a full-size model, of course, but a model built to scale. A model built to scale is smaller than the object it represents, but it has the same shape as the original object.

For example, to build a scale model of a sailboat, a modeler might use a scale of 1 inch to 1 foot. That means that 1 inch of length on the model would represent 1 foot of length on the full-size sailboat. If the real boat were 40 *feet* long, the model would be 40 *inches* long. Of course, a scale of 1 inch to 1 foot is only one of many scales that could be used in building a model.

 Suppose another modeler wanted to make a smaller model of the same sailboat. That modeler might use a scale of $\frac{1}{2}$ inch to 1 foot. Now every $\frac{1}{2}$ inch on the model would represent 1 foot on the full-size boat. Using this scale, how long would the model be of the 40-foot boat? _____

As you probably figured out, the model built to a scale of $\frac{1}{2}$ inch to the foot would be 20 inches long.

SCALES ON GLOBES

Like models, globes can be built to a variety of scales. One common scale is this: One inch equals 500 miles. That means 1 inch on the globe is equal to 500 miles on the earth's surface.

 Suppose you measured the distance between two cities at 2 inches on a globe with a scale of 1 inch to 500 miles. How many miles would there be between the two cities? _____

45

This quiz will help you find out if you have learned the material covered in Chapters 1 through 6.

A. Tell which of the following statements are true and which are false.

1. A globe is the most accurate model of the earth. _____

2. Globes contain more information than flat maps. _____

3. The equator is an imaginary line that runs from the North Pole to the South Pole.

_____

4. Europe and Asia are in the Western Hemisphere. _____

5. When it is 1:00 P.M. in California, it is 4:00 P.M. in New York. _____

6. The United States of America is a continent. _____

7. Distances east and west on a globe are measured from the prime meridian.

_____

8. The letters **N, S, E,** and **W** represent cardinal directions. _____

9. Measurements on a globe are usually given in degrees. _____

10. Lines that run east and west on a globe are latitude lines. _____

1. The

2. The

   calle

3. Figu

   and

4. Land

_____

5. Land

_____

6. Figu

7. Figu

8. The

_____

E. Ansv

1. A glo

   that

2. If you

_____

3. Imagi

   each

Quiz 1

Globes

B. Match each term with its definition.

_____ 1. time zone

_____ 2. equator

_____ 3. axis

_____ 4. globe

a. an imaginary line that runs through the center of the earth

b. an imaginary line around the middle of the earth

c. a model of the earth

d. an area of the world where all places are on the same time

e. one of the earth's hemispheres

C. Identify each of the parts of the globe shown in Figure 1.

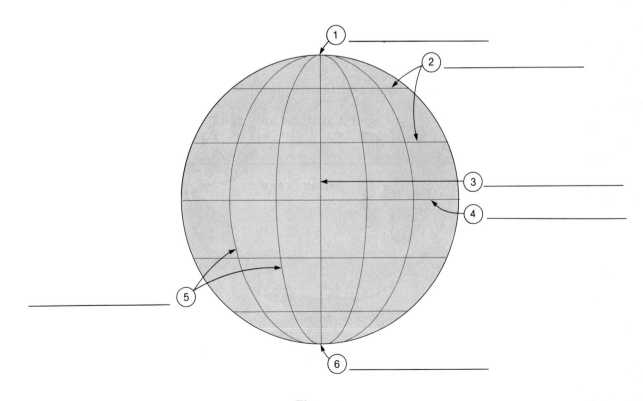

Figure 1

THE MERCATOR PROJECTION

The **Mercator projection** was developed more than 300 years ago (in 1569) by Gerardus Mercator, a Dutch mapmaker. He developed the projection for sailors to aid them in finding their way across the great oceans. Even today sailors and navigators use charts with the Mercator projection because Mercator maps are good for telling directions.

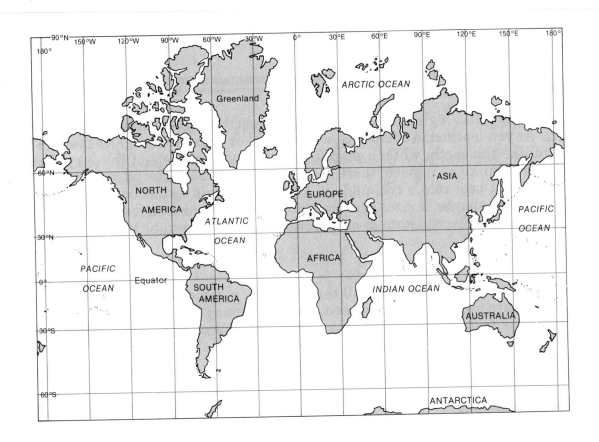

Figure 7.1 A World Map: Mercator Projection

Look at the Mercator map in Figure 7.1 and the globe in Figure 7.2. Compare the parallels and the meridians on the map to those on the globe.

How do the parallels on the Mercator map differ from those on the globe?

_____

_____

How do the meridians on the Mercator map differ from those on the globe?

_____

_____

60 Chapter 7

Figure 7.2   A Globe with Parallels and Meridians

The parallels, or latitude lines, on the Mercator map grow farther apart as the distance from the equator increases. On the globe, the distance between parallels does not change. The meridians, or longitude lines, on the map are evenly spaced straight lines. They would not meet at the poles as the curved meridians on the globe do.

The result of this is that the Mercator projection distorts the *sizes*—but not the shapes—of land and water areas. The farther the land or water area is from the equator, the greater the distortion is.

 Look again at the map in Figure 7.1. Which looks larger, Greenland or South America? _____

Although Greenland looks larger than South America, it is not. Indeed, South America is more than eight times as large as Greenland. (Greenland covers 840,000 square miles; South America, 6,900,000 square miles.)

The important points to remember about the Mercator projection are these:

- Parallels and meridians are straight lines.
- Meridians are evenly spaced all across a map.
- Parallels grow farther apart as the latitude increases.
- Distortion of the sizes of land and water areas is least at the equator and greatest at the poles.

THE MOLLWEIDE PROJECTION

Figure 7.3 shows the **Mollweide projection** [mole WIDE ah], or equal area projection. It is the work of a German astronomer, Karl Mollweide, who developed it in 1825.

Unlike a Mercator map, a Mollweide map shows the true sizes of land and water areas. This makes Mollweide maps good for comparing sizes, such as the areas of Greenland and South America. The Mollweide projection is used on many world maps drawn for special purposes, such as to show where people live or how much rain falls.

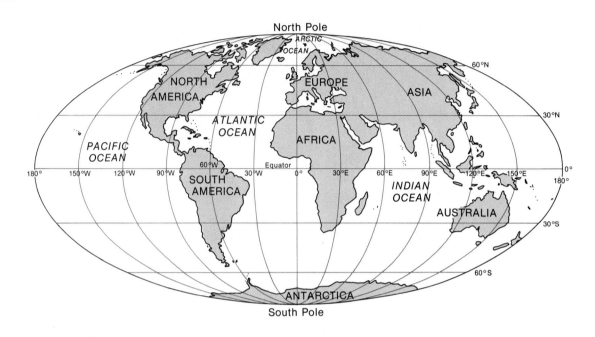

Figure 7.3   A World Map: Mollweide Projection

Compare the Mercator map in Figure 7.1 with the Mollweide map in Figure 7.3. What differences do you notice about the following things:

the shapes of the maps _____

_____

the meridians _____

_____

the parallels _____

_____

The Mollweide map is oval, and the Mercator map is rectangular. On the Mollweide map the meridians, except for the prime meridian, are curved. They meet at the poles. On the Mercator map, meridians are straight and evenly spaced; they don't meet. The parallels on a Mollweide map grow closer together as the distance from the equator increases. The opposite is true on a Mercator map.

The result of these differences is that a Mollweide map distorts the *shapes* of land and water areas. The distortion becomes greater as the distance from the center of the map increases.

The following are important points to remember about the Mollweide projection:

- A Mollweide map is oval shaped.
- Except for the prime meridian, all meridians on a Mollweide map are curved.
- Parallels on a Mollweide map get closer together as their distance from the equator increases.
- Distortion of the shapes of land and water areas increases as the distance from the center of the map increases.

THE INTERRUPTED PROJECTION

No single flat map can show size, shape, direction, and distance accurately. The one that comes closest, however, is drawn with the **interrupted projection,** or broken projection.

An interrupted projection map is nothing more than a Mollweide map with the water areas cut up. Figure 7.4 shows this kind of map.

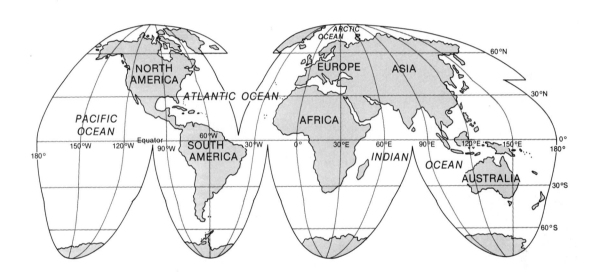

Figure 7.4 A World Map: Interrupted Projection

Cutting up the water areas allows the mapmaker to correct distortions of land area shapes. Of course, the shapes and sizes of water areas become harder to imagine because the water areas have been pulled apart. The interrupted projection, like the Mollweide projection, is used on many maps drawn for special purposes.

DIFFERENT AMOUNTS OF DISTORTION

There is some distortion on all flat maps because they picture a curved earth. Distortion is greatest on a map of the whole earth because all the "sides" of a sphere are flattened out on the map. Therefore, different projections produce world maps that look different from each other. On a map of a small area, such as a state, county, or town, there is very little distortion because the amount that the earth's surface curves is slight in a small area. Maps of small areas drawn with different projections look similar to each other.

HOW CAREFULLY DID YOU READ?

A. Choose the correct completion for each statement.

1. The interrupted projection is

   ☐ a. most like the Mercator projection.

   ☐ b. most like the Mollweide projection.

   ☐ c. like both the Mercator and Mollweide projections.

2. The Mercator projection was developed to help

   ☐ a. sailors.

   ☐ b. globe makers.

   ☐ c. truck drivers.

3. The Mollweide projection is also known as the

   ☐ a. Mercator projection.

   ☐ b. equal area projection.

   ☐ c. broken projection.

4. Mercator maps distort the

   ☐ a. sizes of land areas.

   ☐ b. shapes of land areas.

   ☐ c. sizes and shapes of land areas.

5. Mollweide maps distort the

☐ a. sizes of land areas.

☐ b. shapes of land areas.

☐ c. sizes and shapes of land areas.

6. The interrupted projection cuts up water areas to make a map that is

☐ a. smaller than one with a Mollweide projection.

☐ b. more accurate than a globe.

☐ c. more accurate than one with a Mollweide projection.

B. For each projection, list at least one advantage and one disadvantage.

1. Mercator projection

   Advantage: _____

   Disadvantage: _____

2. Mollweide projection

   Advantage: _____

   Disadvantage: _____

3. Interrupted projection

   Advantage: _____

   Disadvantage: _____

Check your answers on page 136.

Look back at **How Much Do You Already Know?** on page 58. Did you complete each statement correctly? If not, can you do so now?

How Much Do You Already Know?

Choose the correct completion for each statement. If you are not sure about an answer, do not guess.

1. All north and south measurements on the earth's surface start at the

   ☐ a. equator.
   ☐ b. prime meridian.
   ☐ c. International Date Line.

2. All east and west measurements on the earth's surface start at the

   ☐ a. equator.
   ☐ b. prime meridian.
   ☐ c. International Date Line.

3. The most accurate way to locate a place on a map is by use of

   ☐ a. a grid system.
   ☐ b. latitude and longitude lines.
   ☐ c. an index.

4. The grid squares in a grid system are labeled with

   ☐ a. degrees and cardinal directions.
   ☐ b. letters and numbers.
   ☐ c. degrees and letters.

Check your answers on page 136.

Locating Places on a Map

8

 As on a globe, the most accurate way to locate places on a flat map is by latitude and longitude.

LATITUDE LINES

Latitude lines, as you read in Chapter 4, are imaginary lines that run east-west around the earth. Latitude lines are also called parallels because they are always the same distance apart.

Do you remember the name of the most important latitude line? _____

The equator is the most important latitude line. All north and south measurements on the earth's surface start at the equator, which is zero degrees (0°).

Figure 8.1 shows that there are 90° of latitude north of the equator and 90° of latitude south of the equator. The poles are at 90°N and 90°S.

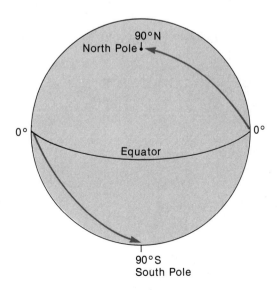

Figure 8.1 Degrees of Latitude North and South of the Equator

LONGITUDE LINES

Longitude lines, or meridians, are imaginary lines that run north-south, from the North Pole to the South Pole. Unlike parallels, meridians are not always the same distance apart. They are farthest apart at the point where they cross the equator. They get closer together as they approach and finally meet at the poles.

Do you remember the name of the most important longitude line?

_____

The prime meridian is the most important longitude line. All east and west measurements on the earth's surface start at the prime meridian, which is zero degrees (0°). There are 180° of longitude east of the prime meridian, and 180° of longitude west of the prime meridian. The imaginary line where east and west longitude meet (180°) is called the International Date Line. See Figure 8.2.

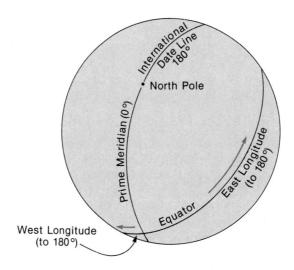

Figure 8.2   Degrees of Longitude East and West of the Prime Meridian

LOCATING PLACES BY LATITUDE AND LONGITUDE

Look at Figure 8.3, which is a map of the continent of North America and surrounding areas.

Find Point **A** on the map. On what latitude lines does Point **A** lie? _____

On what longitude line does Point **A** lie? _____

Point **A** lies on the latitude line at 60°N and on the longitude line at 120°W.

The location of Point **A** is the intersection of the latitude and longitude lines

it lies on. How is that location written? _____

Figure 8.3 North America With Latitude and Longitude Lines

The location of Point **A** is 60°N 120°W. Remember that a location is given with the latitude first, followed by the longitude. Because the letters **N** and **S** always signal locations north and south of the equator, the word *latitude* is not written. Likewise, because the letters **E** and **W** always signal locations east and west of the prime meridian, the word *longitude* is not written.

Notice that the latitude and longitude lines on the map in Figure 8.3 intersect, or cross each other, in a regular pattern. The places where they cross are known as **gridpoints**.

Find gridpoint 40°N 80°W on the map. What point is located there? _____

Point **B** is located at 40°N 80°W.

Of course, not every place is located on one of a map's gridpoints. For example, find Ottawa, the capital of Canada, on the map.

Ottawa lies about halfway between which two latitude lines?

_____ and _____

It also lies about halfway between two longtitude lines. Which two?

_____ and _____

Ottawa lies about halfway between 40°N and 50°N. It is also about halfway between 70°W and 80°W.

How should the approximate location of Ottawa be written? _____

Ottawa is located at about 45°N 75°W. Because it lies about halfway between the latitude lines at 40°N and 50°N, it is at about 45°N. Because it lies about halfway between the longitude lines at 70°W and 80°W, it lies at about 75°W.

To give the location of a place that lies somewhere between latitude and longitude lines, you need to estimate how many degrees from each line that place is. To estimate, you need to know how many degrees separate the latitude and longitude lines on the map you are using. On the map in Figure 8.3, there are 10 degrees between lines. Another map may have 5, 15, 20, or any other number of degrees between lines.

LOCATING PLACES ON A GRID SYSTEM

The most accurate way to locate places on a map is by using latitude and longitude, but it is not the only way. Using a **grid system** is another way.

Figure 8.4, a map of part of the United States, shows one kind of grid system. (Latitude and longitude lines form a kind of grid system, but the one in Figure 8.4 is different.) Here a series of numbers runs across the top and bottom of the map, while a series of letters runs down both sides. The letters and numbers on this grid are located between the lines because they refer to all the space between the lines. (This is different from the way the degrees written on a grid made of latitude and longitude lines name the lines.)

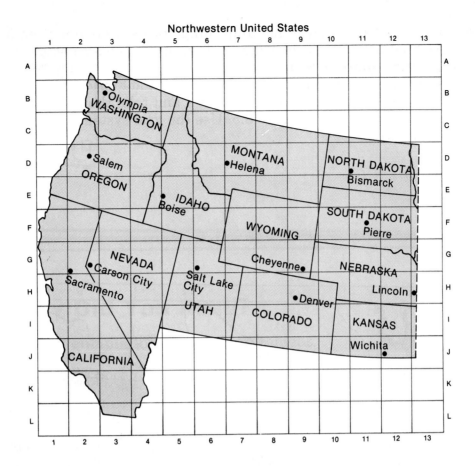

Figure 8.4 The Northwestern United States with a Grid System

To tell the location of a place, find which **grid square** it is in. Then name the grid square by using one letter and one number: the letter straight across from it at the edge of the map, and the number straight above it at the top of the map. For example, the northern tip of Idaho is in grid square **B5**.

Find Olympia, the capital of the state of Washington, on the map in Figure 8.4.

What grid square is Olympia located in? _____

Now find grid square **G6**. What state capital is found in this grid square?

_____

As the map shows, Olympia, Washington, is located in **B3**, while **G6** is the location of Salt Lake City, Utah.

5. On a road map, a letter and number combination, such as **J6**, could identify a

☐ a. latitude.

☐ b. grid square.

☐ c. longitude.

B. Use the map in Figure 8.3 to complete the following statements.

1. The latitude and longitude of Point **C** is _____ .

2. The location at 70°N 150°W is in the state of _____ .

3. The latitude closest to the city of Denver, Colorado, is _____ .

4. The gridpoint closest to Point **D** in Greenland is located at _____ .

5. The city in the United States that lies on the same meridian as Point **B** is

_____ .

6. The location at 20°N 100°W is near a city in the country of _____ .

7. Point **E** is located at about _____ .

8. The city located at about 10°N 84°W is _____ .

C. On the map in Figure 8.4, find the state capital in each of these grid squares.

1. F11 _____   4. J12 _____

2. E5 _____   5. D11 _____

3. D7 _____   6. G2 _____

D. On the map in Figure 8.4, find which grid square each of these state capitals is in.

1. Cheyenne, Wyoming _____   4. Sacramento, California _____

2. Denver, Colorado _____   5. Salem, Oregon _____

3. Lincoln, Nebraska _____

Check your answers on page 136–137.

> Look back at **How Much Do You Already Know?** on page 66. Did you complete each statement correctly? If not, can you do so now?

DID YOU KNOW that the word *map* comes from *mappa*, the ancient Roman word for napkin? In even earlier civilizations, *mappa* meant *signal cloth*. The word *chart* can be traced back to *chartos*, an ancient Greek word meaning *leaf of paper*. Our modern word for a maker of maps and charts is *cartographer*, made up of the old word *chartos* and another ancient Greek word, *graphein*, which meant *to write*.

How Much Do You Already Know?

Choose the correct completion for each statement. If you are not sure about an answer, do not guess.

1. A line like this ---- on a map would likely show

   ☐ a. temperature.
   ☐ b. the boundary between two states.
   ☐ c. a meridian.

2. Features printed in blue on a map are likely to be

   ☐ a. mountains.
   ☐ b. cities.
   ☐ c. bodies of water.

3. In general, words printed in large, bold letters on a map are names of

   ☐ a. important places.
   ☐ b. small towns.
   ☐ c. less important features.

4. The symbol ⊒⊏ on a map would likely indicate a

   ☐ a. railroad.
   ☐ b. bridge.
   ☐ c. city park.

Check your answers on page 137.

Map Language

9

It may sound strange but, yes, you can *read* a map. The reason you can is that maps have a language of their own—a kind of code, or shorthand. However, just as it is impossible to read a book written in, say, German or French without knowing the language, it is impossible to interpret a map accurately without understanding map language.

Fortunately, map language is not hard to understand. Its "vocabulary" consists of lines, colors, patterns, words, and symbols. Some, or all, of these will be part of any map you are likely to use, from a simple map of a neighborhood to a map that shows weather across the country, or one that pictures a part of the world in great detail.

LINES

Lines on maps serve several purposes. Broken lines, such as the following, may be used to mark political boundaries between countries, states, or counties.

Broken lines: — — · · — — · ·   — · — · —   - - - - - -

Figure 9.1   The Continental United States With Broken Lines for State Borders

Figure 9.1 on page 77 shows the forty-eight states in the United States that share borders. Notice that the borders between states are drawn with broken lines. The location of D.C., is shown with a ⊛.

Unbroken lines are used to show latitude and longitude lines on a map or a globe. Figure 9.2 is like Figure 9.1 with the addition of unbroken longitude and latitude lines.

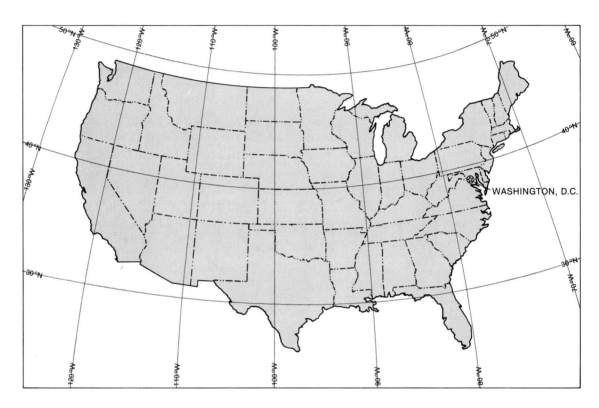

Figure 9.2   The Continental United States With Unbroken Lines for Latitude/Longitude

 What is the approximate latitude and longitude of Washington, D.C.?

_____ (If you have forgotten how to express latitude and

longitude, refer back to Chapter 8.)

Washington, D.C., is located at approximately 40°N 80°W.
Unbroken lines are also used to draw isolines. An **isoline** shows all the places on a map where the temperature, rainfall, or altitude is the same. (The prefix *iso-* comes from the Greek word *isos,* which means *equal,* or *identical.*)

The isolines on the map in Figure 9.3 on page 79 are called **isotherms** because they indicate temperature. At every point along each isotherm the temperature is the same.

For example, Figure 9.3 shows that at a certain time, everywhere along both isotherms marked **40**, the temperature was 40 degrees Fahrenheit (40°F). At each point on the isotherms marked **50**, the temperature was 50°F. Temperatures in places between the 40° and 50° isotherms ranged between 40°F and 50°F.

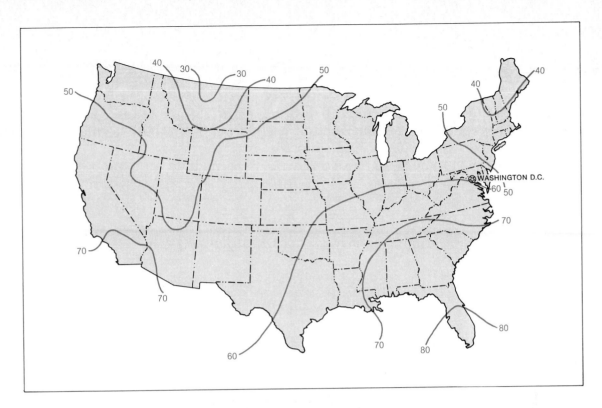

Figure 9.3   The Continental United States With Isotherms

 According to the map in Figure 9.3, what was the approximate temperature in Washington, D.C.? _____

The temperature in Washington was about 60°F.

When an isoline is used to show altitude, or height above sea level, it is called a **contour line.** To show the altitude of the hill in Figure 9.4 on a flat map, a **cartographer,** or mapmaker, would use contour lines.

Figure 9.4   A Hill

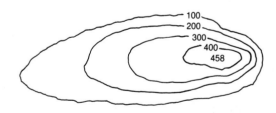

Figure 9.5   A Hill Represented by Contour Lines

Figure 9.5 shows how the hill would look on a flat map. Notice that the steeper the slope of the hill is, the closer together the contour lines are.

 How many feet above sea level is the highest point on the hill in Figure 9.5?

_____

The peak of the hill is 458 feet above sea level.

COLORS

Many maps are quite colorful. In fact, some maps—especially older ones—are considered works of art, and are highly prized by collectors. But colors are not used to make maps look pretty. Rather, various colors are used to identify particular features.

On some maps blue indicates bodies of water, such as oceans, lakes, and rivers. Brown may show land areas. Red and black are often used to point out features made by people—roads, buildings, factories, airports, and so forth.

On other maps color indicates altitude. These maps include an explanation similar to this one.

white	land below sea level
green	land from sea level to 1,000 feet
yellow	land from 1,000 to 2,000 feet
tan	land from 2,000 to 5,000 feet
orange	land from 5,000 to 10,000 feet
dark brown	land over 10,000 feet above sea level

PATTERNS

Many maps that are not printed in color use patterns or designs to show altitude. A group of patterns that indicate altitude might look something like this.

land below sea level	
sea level to 1,000 feet	
1,000 to 2,000 feet	
2,000 to 5,000 feet	
5,000 to 10,000 feet	
above 10,000 feet	

WORDS

Words are used on maps to label important places and features such as oceans, mountains, countries, parks, roads, buildings, and so on. In general, the larger or more important a place or feature is, the larger its name is on a map.

Look at the map in Figure 9.6 on page 81. Which is the most important city shown on the map? _____

Which is the least important, or smallest, city shown on the map? _____

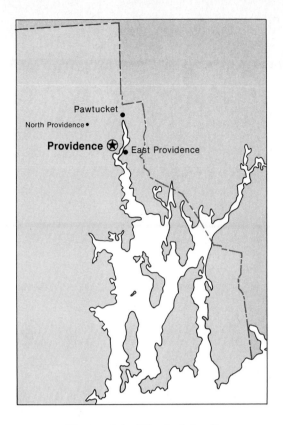

Figure 9.6   Rhode Island

The most important city is the one whose name is in the largest, boldest print—Providence. The least important, or smallest city is North Providence. Its name is in the smallest print.

On some maps names of places and features are printed in color to make them stand out. It is common to see the names of bodies of water printed in blue and the names of forests and parks printed in green. Places of interest, such as museums, historic buildings, and universities, often appear in red.

SYMBOLS

A **symbol**, you may already know, is something that stands for another thing. For example, +, −, ×, and ÷ are symbols for addition, subtraction, multiplication, and division. Symbols allow a lot of information to be shown in a small area.

Many symbols are so clear that their meanings are easily understood. However, different maps may use different clear symbols for the same feature. For instance, on one road map a campground may be indicated by a ⛺, but on another map, by a ⛺. This symbol shows the cardinal directions on some maps. Other maps use this symbol ↑ or some other symbol to show which way north is.

What might be an appropriate and clear map symbol for each of the following features?

an airport ☐   a hospital ☐   a church ☐

An airport could be represented by a ✈; a hospital, by a ✚; and a church by a 🏠.

You may, however, come across symbols whose meanings are not so evident. A map might use a ▲ to indicate a campground, or a ⊖ or a **T** to show the location of a subway. In cases like this, you need to look at the map's legend. A **legend** is a key that explains all the symbols used on a particular map. You can usually find the legend at the bottom of a map. Figure 9.7 shows an example of a legend from a road map.

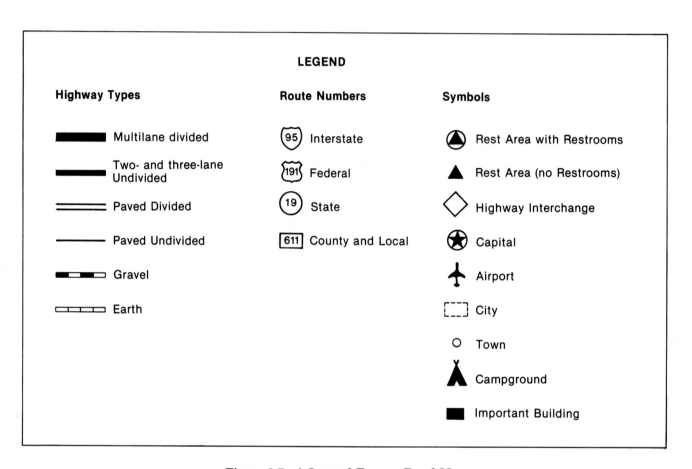

Figure 9.7   A Legend From a Road Map

How Carefully Did You Read?

A. Choose the correct completion for each statement.

1. Unbroken lines on a map are likely to indicate

   ☐ a. political boundaries.

   ☐ b. bodies of water.

   ☐ c. latitude and longitude lines.

2. The points on an isoline

   ☐ a. all have the same value.

   ☐ b. have different values.

   ☐ c. have a range of values.

3. Color is used on maps to

   ☐ a. identify certain features.

   ☐ b. make maps more interesting.

   ☐ c. make maps beautiful.

4. On maps, places and features are labeled with

   ☐ a. lines.

   ☐ b. words.

   ☐ c. colors.

5. A map symbol for a railroad would likely be

   ☐ a. ========

   ☐ b. +++++++++++

   ☐ c. ⬭

B. Use the legend in Figure 9.7 on page 82 to complete the following statements.

1. The symbol for a capital city is

   ☐ a. ○
   ☐ b. ✪
   ☐ c. ⸾⸽

2. The route number on a state highway is shown by the symbol

   ☐ a. ⑨⑤
   ☐ b. 611
   ☐ c. ⑲

3. The symbol ◇ indicates a

   ☐ a. campground.
   ☐ b. rest area.
   ☐ c. highway interchange.

4. A highway rest area that has restrooms is shown by

   ☐ a. ◉

   ☐ b. ▲

   ☐ c. ✪

5. The symbol ■ indicates a(n)

   ☐ a. campground.
   ☐ b. airport.
   ☐ c. important building.

6. A road that is drawn with this kind of line ▬▬▭▬▭▬ is

   ☐ a. a multilane, divided road.
   ☐ b. a paved, divided road.
   ☐ c. a gravel road.

C. Use the legend in Figure 9.7 on page 82 and the map in Figure 9.8 to answer the following.

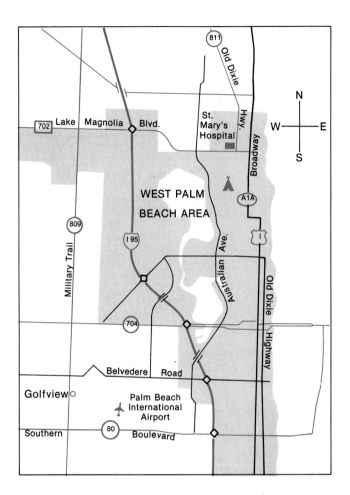

Figure 9.8   West Palm Beach, Florida Area

1. State Highway 809 is also known by what other name? _____

2. How many highway interchanges on I-95 does the map show? _____

3. What is located at the intersection of Lake Magnolia Boulevard and Old Dixie Highway?

_____

4. The campground shown on the map lies

   (a) south of what road? _____

   (b) east of what road? _____

   (c) west of what road? _____

5. What is the name of the road just

    (a) north of the airport? _____

    (b) south of the airport? _____

6. According to the legend, what kind of place is Golfview? _____

Check your answers on page 137.

> Look back at **How Much Do You Already Know?** on page 76. Did you complete each statement correctly? If not, can you do so now?

DID YOU KNOW that the first person to put north at the top of maps was an Egyptian named Ptolemy [TAL ah me], about the year 150 A.D.? Today nearly all maps put north at the top. Ptolemy began putting north at the top of his maps simply because both the Mediterranean Sea and Greece, important areas to the Egyptians, lay to the north of Egypt. Later, during the Middle Ages (about 500–1450 A.D.), many maps were drawn with the Holy Land, which was important to the Crusaders, at the top and Europe at the bottom. That meant that east was at the top of those maps.

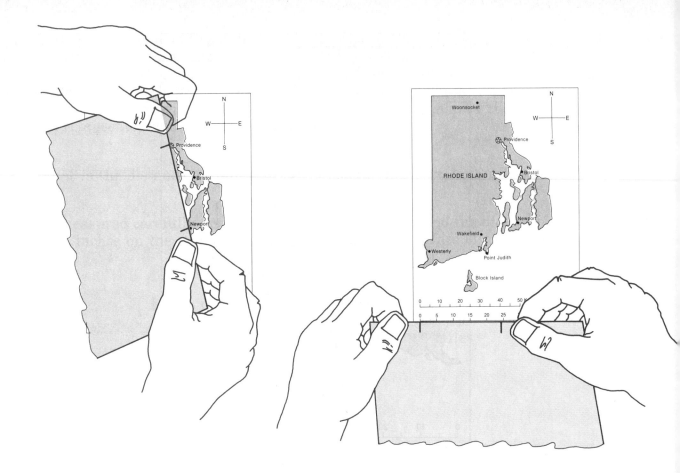

Illustration of Steps in Using Graphic Scales

 According to the map and graphic scale in Figure 10.2, about how many miles

separate Providence and Newport, Rhode Island? _____

What is that distance in kilometers? _____

If you measured carefully, you found that the distance between the two cities is about 25 miles, or about 40 kilometers.

 According to the same map and graphic scale, about how many miles is Prov-

idence from Woonsocket, Rhode Island? _____

About how many kilometers is that? _____

Providence is about 12 miles, or 20 kilometers, from Woonsocket.

REPRESENTATIVE FRACTIONS

The third kind of map scale is a **representative fraction**, or **RF**, as it is sometimes called. On a map, an RF looks something like this:

1:62,500   or this: $\dfrac{1}{62,500}$

In an RF, the numeral **1** always means one unit of measure on the map. The other number tells the number of units of measure on the earth's surface. An RF of 1:62,500 means that one unit of measure on the map equals 62,500 equal units of measure on the surface of the earth. The unit can be any length at all. For example, 1 centimeter on the map would represent 62,500 centimeters on the surface of the earth. (Many countries use centimeters instead of inches as a unit of measure. One inch equals 2.54 centimeters; one centimeter equals 0.39 inches.)

 On a map with an RF of 1:62,500, how much distance on the surface of the earth

would 1 inch on the map represent? _____

An inch on the map would represent 62,500 inches on the surface of the earth.

Some maps have both a graphic scale and a representative fraction. Look at Figure 10.3, a scale map of Puerto Rico. Notice the figures 1:1,000,000 above the graphic scale. That is the RF. Every unit of distance on the map represents 1 million units of the same distance on the surface of the earth. One inch on the map represents 1 million inches, or about 16 miles, on the surface of the earth. Similarly, one centimeter on the map represents 1 million centimeters on the surface of the earth, or 10 kilometers.

 According to the graphic scale in Figure 10.3, about what is the distance, in

miles, between San Juan and Arecibo, Puerto Rico? _____

What is the distance in kilometers? _____

The distance is about 39 miles, or about 63 kilometers.

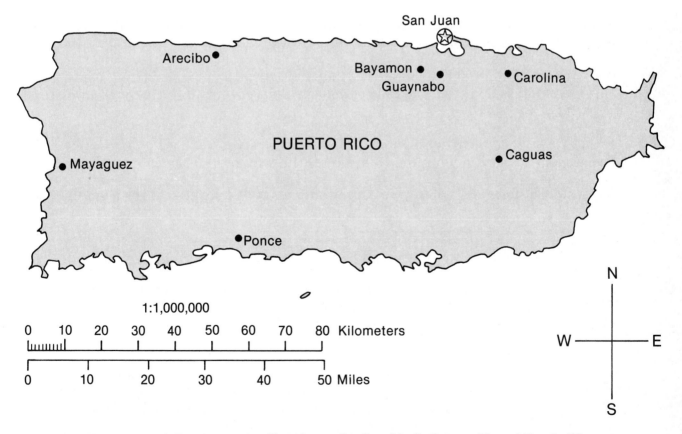

Figure 10.3   A Representative Fraction and a Graphic Scale on a Map of Puerto Rico

LARGE-SCALE AND SMALL-SCALE MAPS

Maps can show the earth with great detail or with little detail. If a map shows a lot of detail, it is called a **large-scale map;** if it doesn't show much detail, it is called a **small-scale map**.

Figures 10.4 and 10.5 show the difference between large-scale and small-scale maps. The large-scale map in Figure 10.4 shows a small area of Washington, D.C., in detail. The small-scale map in Figure 10.5 is the same size as the map in Figure 10.4. It shows a larger area, including Washington, D.C., but it doesn't show much detail.

Figure 10.4 A Large-scale Map of Washington D.C.

Figure 10.5 A Small-scale Map of the Washington D.C. Area

A map with an RF of 1:62,500, like the map in Figure 10.4, is considered to be a large-scale map. One unit of measure on such a map represents relatively few units of measure on the surface of the earth.

A map with an RF of 1:1,000,000, like the map in Figure 10.5, is considered to be a small-scale map. On small-scale maps, one unit of measure represents a relatively great distance on the surface of the earth.

 Imagine that you are planning to drive all the way across the country, from Maine to California. To plan your trip, would you use a large-scale or a small-scale map? _____

Imagine that you are in a strange town and that you have to drive from one side of town to the other. Would a large-scale or a small-scale map be more useful to you? _____

To plan a trip across the country, a small-scale map would be better because it would show a lot of area without too much detail. To see how to get across a strange town, however, it would be better to use a large-scale map because it would show a lot of detail.

How Carefully Did You Read?

A. Choose the correct completion for each statement.

1. A map scale shows how distances on a map compare to distances on

   ☐ a. any other map.
   ☐ b. a map not drawn to scale.
   ☐ c. the surface of the earth.

2. The expression **RF** is an abbreviation that stands for

   ☐ a. the word *map*.
   ☐ b. any small-scale map.
   ☐ c. a kind of map scale.

3. If a map has a scale in which 1 inch equals 400 miles, two cities 3 inches apart on the map are actually

   ☐ a. 12 miles apart.
   ☐ b. 300 miles apart.
   ☐ c. 1,200 miles apart.

4. The kind of map scale that can show most clearly both miles and kilometers is a

   ☐ a. words and figures scale.
   ☐ b. graphic scale.
   ☐ c. representative fraction.

5. If a map scale is expressed as 1:400,000, then 1 inch on the map equals

☐ a. 1 mile on the surface of the earth.

☐ b. 400,000 inches on the surface of the earth.

☐ c. 400,000 miles on the surface of the earth.

6. This scale [scale bar: 0 100 200 300 400 Mi / 0 160 320 480 640 Km] shows that a distance of 200 kilometers is

☐ a. longer than 200 miles.

☐ b. the same length as 200 miles.

☐ c. shorter than 200 miles.

7. This scale [scale bar: 0 100 200 Miles] is 1 inch long. In words and figures, it means

☐ a. 1 inch = 1 mile.

☐ b. 1 inch = 100 miles.

☐ c. 1 inch = 200 miles.

8. A large-scale map shows

☐ a. a small area in great detail.

☐ b. a large area with little detail.

☐ c. the whole world.

B. Use Figures 10.1 through 10.5 to complete the following statements.

1. The distance between Abilene and Tyler, Texas, is about _____ miles.

2. Two cities in Texas are 200 miles apart. The distance between them in kilometers is

_____ .

3. The distance between Westerly and Woonsocket, Rhode Island, is about

_____ miles or _____ kilometers.

4. The shortest distance between Bristol and the western border of Rhode Island is

about _____ miles or _____ kilometers.

5. The distance between Mayaguez and Ponce in Puerto Rico is about _____

miles or _____ kilometers.

6. According to the graphic scale in Figure 10.3, a distance of 50 kilometers is about the same as _____ miles.

7. According to Figure 10.4, on a map with an RF of 1:62,500, 1 inch represents a distance of about _____ on the surface of the earth.

8. According to Figure 10.5, 1 inch equals about 16 miles on a map with an RF of _____ .

Check your answers on page 137.

Look back at **How Much Do You Already Know?** on page 88. Did you complete each statement correctly? If not, can you do so now?

DID YOU KNOW that someone once said we make maps because we are very small creatures in a very big world? We want to see much more of the earth than our eyes can take in. Maps help us to do this. They show us in a very small space what the huge world looks like.

How Much Do You Already Know?

Choose the correct completion for each statement. If you are not sure about an answer, do not guess.

1. The legend on a map explains the meanings of the map's

   ☐ a. symbols.
   ☐ b. isotherms.
   ☐ c. labels.

2. On a weather map, if the symbol for snow is ⬚ , the symbol for flurries would likely be

   ☐ a. ⬚
   ☐ b. ⬚
   ☐ c. ⬚

3. This symbol ▼▼ on a weather map likely indicates

   ☐ a. a campground.
   ☐ b. heavy rain.
   ☐ c. a cold front.

4. The symbols on a resources and products map are usually drawn

   ☐ a. to actual size.
   ☐ b. to scale.
   ☐ c. rather large.

Check your answers on page 137.

Legends

11

A symbol, as you read in Chapter 9, is something that stands for another thing. Symbols are common on maps because they tell a lot in very little space. When a map uses symbols, the meanings of the symbols are explained in a legend.

Figure 11.1 is a small part of a road map. It shows an area that includes part of Buffalo, New York. Notice that a broken line like this ___ __ __ ___ __ __ ___ shows the boundary between Canada and the United States.

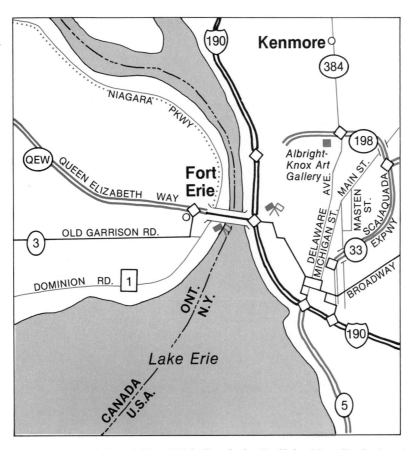

Figure 11.1 A Road Map With Symbols (Buffalo, New York Area)

Among other things, the legend for this map would tell you that (a) this symbol ⚒ stands for a customs station, (b) a part of a road drawn this way ⎓ crosses a bridge, and (c) a road drawn this way ⁚⁚⁚⁚ is a scenic highway.

The map shows two customs stations. Where are they? _____

_____

What is the name of the scenic highway shown on the map? _____

_____

There is one customs station at each end of the bridge that connects Canada and the United States. The map shows that the Niagara Parkway is a scenic highway.

Road maps are not the only kinds of maps that have legends. Any kind of map that uses symbols has a legend to explain those symbols.

WEATHER MAPS

Figure 11.2 is a weather map. It shows what the weather was like in part of the United States on December 2 in a recent year.

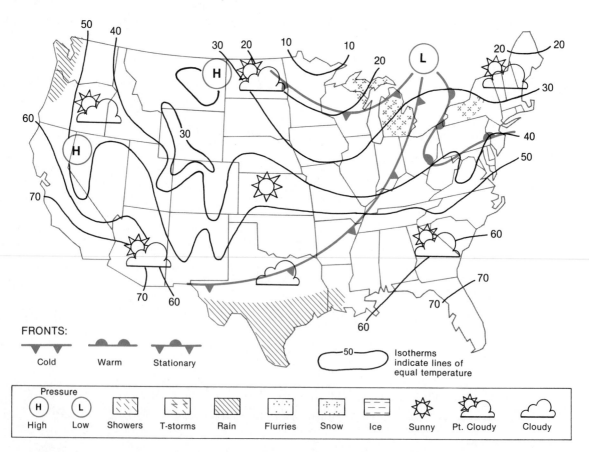

Figure 11.2   A Weather Map of the Continental United States Showing One Day's Weather

The temperatures are shown by isotherms. (You read about isotherms in Chapter 9.) Other information about the weather is shown by symbols that are explained in the legend at the bottom of the map. (The symbols on the map in Figure 11.2 are commonly used on weather maps.)

Some of the symbols on the map show where weather fronts were on December 2. (A front is the leading edge of a mass of air.) For example, the legend shows that this symbol ▼▼ represents a **cold front**.

How many cold fronts does the map in Figure 11.2 show? _____

Besides cold fronts, what other kind of front does the map show? _____

The map shows two cold fronts and a **warm front**.
Areas of high and low pressure are indicated by these symbols: (H) and (L).

How many areas with high pressure does the map show? _____

How many areas with low pressure does the map show? _____

The map shows two high pressure areas and one low pressure area.
As the legend shows, there are symbols to indicate where there was **precipitation**—showers, thunderstorms, rain, flurries, snow, or ice. For example, the legend shows that this symbol ⬚ indicates snow.

The map shows that there were two kinds of precipitation on December 2. Which two kinds does it show? _____ and _____

The map shows that there was rain in two different areas and snow in three different areas. Still other symbols report the condition of the skies—sunny, partly cloudy, or cloudy.

In the area right in the middle of the map, the skies were sunny. What were the skies like in most of the rest of the country? _____

In most of the country where it was not sunny, the skies were partly cloudy. This symbol 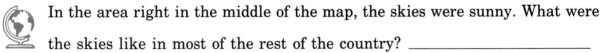 shows that. It appears five times on the map.

Some weather maps show something about conditions in an area over a period of time. The map of North America in Figure 11.3 on page 102 is such a map. It shows the mean annual temperature. (**Mean temperature** is the average of all the temperatures recorded over a period of time.)

The legend explains the meanings of the symbols, or patterns, on the map.

3. The two kinds of precipitation shown on the map are _____ and

   _____ .

4. The map shows two _____ fronts.

5. The map shows that in the Southeast the skies were _____ and the

   temperature was about _____ °F.

6. In the Northeast the skies were _____ and the temperatures ranged

   from about _____ °F up to about 40°F.

Check your answers on page 137.

Look back at **How Much Do You Already Know?** on page 98. Did
you complete each statement correctly? If not, can you do so now?

DID YOU KNOW that enough road maps are produced every year in the United States to give one to every man, woman, and child there?

How Much Do You Already Know?

Choose the correct completion for each statement. If you are not sure about an answer, do not guess.

1. In general, a map of a very large area shows

   ☐ a. no details.
   ☐ b. few details.
   ☐ c. many details.

2. Compared to the area a map shows, the area a map inset shows is

   ☐ a. smaller.
   ☐ b. the same size.
   ☐ c. larger.

3. Ordinarily maps and their insets are drawn

   ☐ a. without scales.
   ☐ b. to different scales.
   ☐ c. to the same scale.

4. If the purpose of a map inset is to show locations and not distances, the inset may

   ☐ a. be drawn to a large scale.
   ☐ b. not be drawn to scale.
   ☐ c. be drawn to a small scale.

Check your answers on page 137.

110

Insets

12

One important decision any cartographer is faced with is what details to include on a map and what details to leave off. Since all maps are smaller than the area they show, it is impossible to include every detail and feature.

Generally speaking, the more area a map shows, the less detail it has. For instance, a map of North America that is 3 feet by 2 feet can include only large features. It would likely show the boundaries of countries, states, and provinces. It would probably also show the locations of large cities, rivers, lakes, and mountains.

On the other hand, another map 3 feet by 2 feet of one city block can include much more detail. Here you are likely to find every building, streetlight, and traffic signal—perhaps even fire hydrants and trees!

However, with insets, mapmakers can include extra details on a map that otherwise would not be able to show them. An **inset** picks up a small area of a map and blows it up in greater detail.

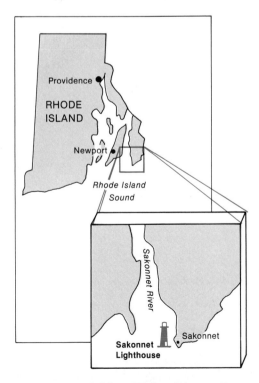

Figure 12.1   A Map With a Picture Inset

PICTURE INSETS

Figure 12.1 on page 111 shows a map with a picture inset. Maps with insets like this one are common in newspapers and news magazines. This one could go with an article about a lighthouse.

 What state does the map show? _____

What is the name of the main feature pictured in the inset?

_____

The map shows Rhode Island. The main feature in the inset is the picture of Sakonnet Lighthouse.

The map is not very large. It doesn't allow enough detail to include the Sakonnet Lighthouse. The square inset, however, shows where Sakonnet is and has a drawing of the lighthouse there—not to scale, of course. The small square on the map shows which part of the state is blown up in the inset. That way you can see where the lighthouse is in Rhode Island.

Notice that the inset in Figure 12.1, like many insets, is not drawn to scale. If it were, the Sakonnet River, for example, would be wider. The inset's purpose is to show the *location* of the lighthouse, not actual distances within Rhode Island.

ROAD MAP INSETS

Road maps often have insets to show certain areas in more detail. Some are drawn to scale; some are not. Figure 12.2 is a road map of part of Louisiana with an inset on the left.

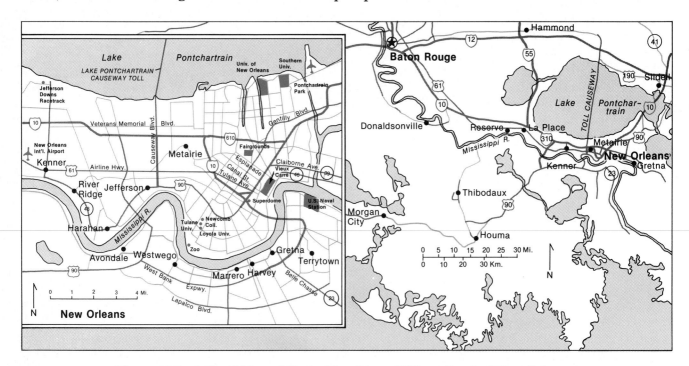

Figure 12.2   A Road Map of Part of Louisiana With an Inset of New Orleans

Look at the main map first. It shows two large cities, Baton Rouge and New Orleans. A highway connects Baton Rouge and New Orleans. The number of the highway is printed

inside a figure like this ⛊. That figure shows that the road is an interstate highway.

What is the number of the highway that connects Baton Rouge and New Orleans? _____

The number of the highway is 10. Because it is an interstate highway, it is called Interstate 10 or I-10.

The inset in the road map of Louisiana shows New Orleans in more detail than the main map can. The inset is also a road map.

 There are two different interstate highways shown in the inset. What are those interstate highways called? _____ and _____

The two interstate highways shown in the inset are I-10 and I-610.

The inset shows that I-10 runs right through New Orleans. That's one of the details on the inset that the main map does not show. The main map simply shows that I-10 goes *to* New Orleans.

Find the graphic scales on the main map and on the inset. (You read about graphic scales in Chapter 10.) The two scales are different. Use a ruler to find out how many miles 1 inch represents on each scale.

 On the map of Louisiana, how many miles are there to an inch?

_____

In the inset of New Orleans, about how many miles are there to an inch?

_____

On the Louisiana map, 1 inch represents 30 miles. In the inset, 1 inch represents only about 4 miles. The inset is drawn to a larger scale than the map.

INSETS WITHIN INSETS

On some maps, there are insets within insets. The second inset shows something about the first in even more detail. Figure 12.3 on page 114 shows the inset from Figure 12.2 with another inset.

 What does the new inset in Figure 12.3 show? _____

The new inset shows Central New Orleans.

The inset of Central New Orleans blows up a part of New Orleans. Notice, however, that there is no marking that shows which part of New Orleans is blown up in the new inset. (Recall that the map in Figure 12.1 has a square on it to show what part of Rhode Island is pictured in its inset.) There is a way to find out which part of New Orleans is blown up. You need to look for features that are shown in both insets.

Notice that Interstate 10 appears in both insets. The part of I-10 shown in the Central New Orleans inset is quite close to the Mississippi River. Find the part of I-10 nearest to the river in the other inset. It's on the east, or right, side of the New Orleans inset.

In the Central New Orleans inset, look at the area between I-10 and the Mississippi River. Vieux Carre, the French Quarter of New Orleans, is there. It has the shape of a rectangle.

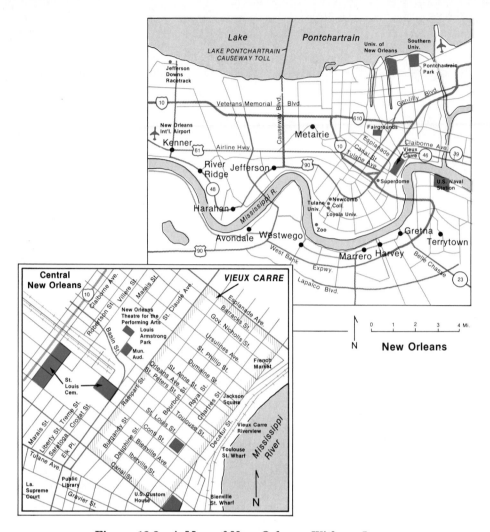

Figure 12.3   A Map of New Orleans With an Inset

Finally, look at the same area between I-10 and the Mississippi River in the New Orleans inset. Do you see the rectangle that represents Vieux Carre? If you do, then you have found the part of New Orleans that is blown up in the Central New Orleans inset.

Compare the way Vieux Carre is shown in the two insets.

 What details about Vieux Carre are shown in the Central New Orleans inset that are not shown in the New Orleans inset? _____

_____

Among other things, the Central New Orleans inset shows the streets in Vieux Carre. The other inset doesn't show any detail about Vieux Carre at all.

Because the area shown in the Central New Orleans inset is so small, it is not drawn to scale. Like the purpose of the inset in the map of Rhode Island, this inset's purpose is to show locations, not distances. Insets like this one are quite useful to people who need directions for walking or driving on local streets.

How Carefully Did You Read?

A. Choose the correct completion for each statement.

1. No maps show all the details in an area because

   ☐ a. cartographers decide to leave them off.
   ☐ b. maps are smaller than the area they show.
   ☐ c. details cannot be drawn to scale.

2. When a map has an inset, the purpose of the inset is usually to show an area in

   ☐ a. more detail than the map does.
   ☐ b. as much detail as the map does.
   ☐ c. less detail than the map does.

3. A likely inset for a city map would show

   ☐ a. the downtown area of the city.
   ☐ b. the whole state that the city is part of.
   ☐ c. the country that the city is part of.

4. Compared to a map's scale, an inset's scale is

   ☐ a. smaller.
   ☐ b. the same size.
   ☐ c. larger.

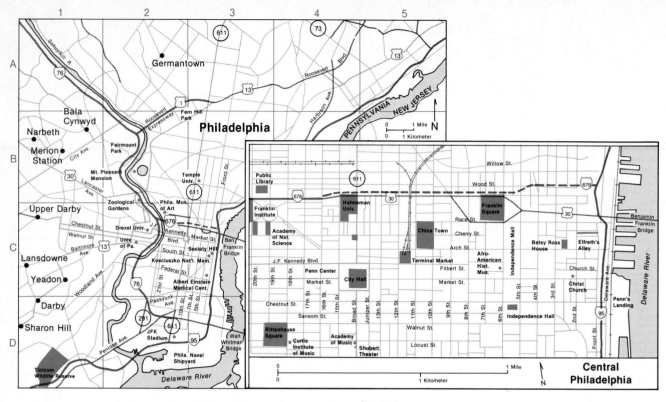

Figure 12.4 A Map With an Inset

B. Use Figure 12.4 to complete the following statements.

1. Figure 12.4 is a map of _____ with an inset that shows

   _____ .

2. Two features that are shown both on the map and in the inset are _____

   and _____ .

3. According to the graphic scale on the map, 1 inch on the map represents a distance

   of a little less than _____ miles.

4. According to the graphic scale on the map inset, 1 inch on the inset represents about

   _____ of a mile.

5. The area shown on the map inset is in grid squares _____ and

   _____ on the map.

Check your answers on page 137.

Look back at **How Much Do You Already Know?** on page 110. Did
you complete each statement correctly? If not, can you do so now?

DID YOU KNOW that when the United States Army invaded North Africa in 1942 during World War II, the soldiers took 110 tons of maps ashore with them when they landed? Within four months, another 400 tons were brought ashore. Before the battle was over, more than 10 million maps had been used.

How Much Do You Already Know?

Choose the correct completion for each statement. If you are not sure about an answer, do not guess.

1. An example of a general reference map is a

   ☐ a. weather map.
   ☐ b. road map.
   ☐ c. population map.

2. A special purpose map gives information about

   ☐ a. only one topic.
   ☐ b. a few special topics.
   ☐ c. many different topics.

3. A climate map of a continent shows information about the weather on that continent

   ☐ a. at a certain moment.
   ☐ b. on a particular day.
   ☐ c. over a long period of time.

4. Comparing a country's population map to its annual rainfall map might help you find out why some areas have

   ☐ a. a lot of rain.
   ☐ b. few people.
   ☐ c. rivers.

Check your answers on page 137.

Special Purpose Maps

13

In Chapters 1 through 12 you studied several different kinds of maps. They included **general reference maps,** which show many different features. Road maps, for example, are general reference maps.

Besides roads, what are three other features a road map might show?

_____ , _____ , and _____

A road map might show any of a number of things. Among them are state borders, cities, parks, campgrounds, airports, and buildings.

In Chapter 11 you studied maps that were each drawn to show only one kind of information: weather, temperatures, products and resources, or precipitation. Maps like those are called **special purpose maps.** Each has one, special purpose. Each gives information about only one topic.

There are countless kinds of special purpose maps. Treasure maps and maps that show battle sites are special purpose maps. Still others show where ancient civilizations were and where people of various religions live. The paths migrating birds take, the places accidents often occur, and areas where a certain disease is common can all be shown on special purpose maps.

In this chapter, you will take a look at a few more special purpose maps.

A CLIMATE MAP

A climate map is something like a weather map. There is a difference between them, though. A weather map tells about weather conditions on a particular day. A climate map tells about weather conditions over a long period of time.

Figure 13.1 on page 120 is a climate map of the whole United States. (Notice that Alaska and Hawaii are not shown in their actual locations.)

The legend shows how many different climate regions there are in the United States. It also describes each one.

According to the legend in Figure 13.1, how many climate regions are there

in the United States? _____

The legend shows nine climate regions in the United States.

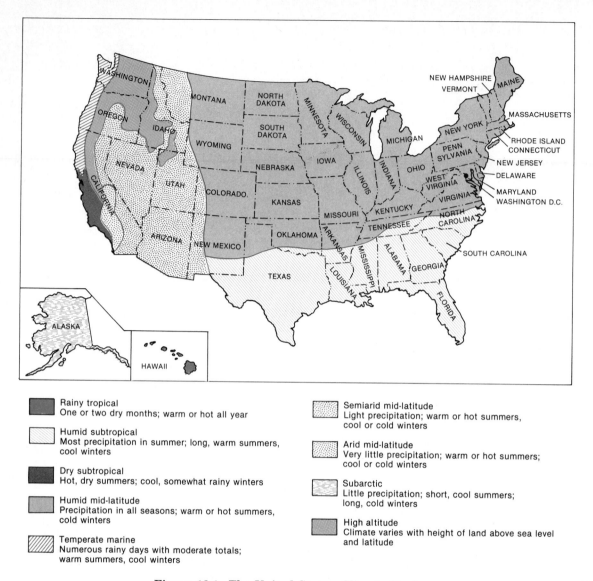

Figure 13.1 The United States: Climate Regions

Rainy tropical
One or two dry months; warm or hot all year

Humid subtropical
Most precipitation in summer; long, warm summers, cool winters

Dry subtropical
Hot, dry summers; cool, somewhat rainy winters

Humid mid-latitude
Precipitation in all seasons; warm or hot summers, cold winters

Temperate marine
Numerous rainy days with moderate totals; warm summers, cool winters

Semiarid mid-latitude
Light precipitation; warm or hot summers, cool or cold winters

Arid mid-latitude
Very little precipitation; warm or hot summers; cool or cold winters

Subarctic
Little precipitation; short, cool summers; long, cold winters

High altitude
Climate varies with height of land above sea level and latitude

If you compare the patterns on the map, you'll see that no other state has the same climate as Hawaii. The same is true of Alaska. Read the descriptions of those two climates in the legend.

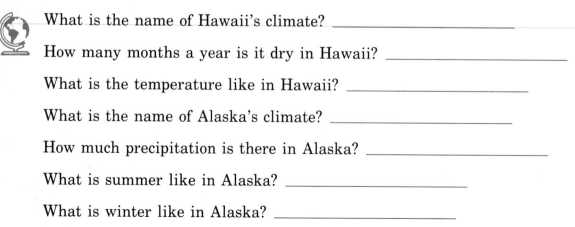

What is the name of Hawaii's climate? _____

How many months a year is it dry in Hawaii? _____

What is the temperature like in Hawaii? _____

What is the name of Alaska's climate? _____

How much precipitation is there in Alaska? _____

What is summer like in Alaska? _____

What is winter like in Alaska? _____

The climate in Hawaii is called rainy tropical. It is dry only one or two months a year there, and it is always warm or hot. In Alaska the climate is called subarctic. There is very little precipitation. Summers are short and cool there; winters are long and cold.

A climate map like the one shown in Figure 13.1 is useful for making comparisons.

 In the United States, how does the winter temperature in the Northeast compare to the winter temperature in the Southeast? _____

Is the climate in Virginia more like the climate in Alabama or in Kansas?

_____

Winter in the Northeast is colder than winter in the Southeast. Virginia's climate is more like Kansas's than Alabama's.

Find your state on the map in Figure 13.1. Read the description of its climate in the legend. Does the description agree with your experience of the climate where you live?

DID YOU KNOW that collecting maps is a growing hobby? Some people collect maps of a single area—their own state or city, for example. Others collect only certain kinds of maps—old road maps, for example, or charts used by sailors. Not only is collecting maps an absorbing hobby, it can be profitable as well. Rare maps are in great demand all over the world. Recently, a 350-year-old chart of the Americas, Africa, and Europe, drawn by a Portuguese cartographer, brought more than $600,000 at auction. A 400-year-old atlas, put together in Venice, sold for more than $1 million!

COMPARING SPECIAL PURPOSE MAPS

Sometimes it is possible to find a relationship between information from two different special purpose maps.

Compare the two maps of Africa. As you saw, Figure 13.2 shows a large area in the north with little rainfall. In about the same place in Figure 13.3, you saw that there are very few people, if any.

 What might the relationship be between those two facts? _____

_____

You probably guessed that there is so little rain in that area that there is not enough water for many, if any, people to live there. If you did, you were right. That area is the Sahara Desert.

Compare rainfall and population in other parts of Africa. Notice that, for the most part, people live where there is at least 10 to 20 inches of rain per year. Also, in general, the areas with the most people have a lot of rain. That makes sense because a large population needs more water than a small one.

According to the maps, there are some areas in Africa with a lot of people, but little rain. At first that doesn't seem to make sense, but water may come from other sources than rain in those areas.

 If an area has little rain, how might it get enough water to allow people to live

there? _____

_____

Water may be piped in to dry areas, or there may be rivers that flow in from areas with more rain.

It's possible to learn a lot by studying different special purpose maps of one area. As noted, sometimes you can see relationships between different kinds of information. However, sometimes two facts from different maps don't seem to go together. When that happens, it's a good idea to look for more information. There may be more to the story than the maps show.

How Carefully Did You Read?

A. Choose the correct completion for each statement.

1. A road map would probably *not* show

   ☐ a. the locations of cities.
   ☐ b. climate regions.
   ☐ c. state lines.

2. To compare average household incomes in different parts of a state, it would be best to use a

   ☐ a. special purpose map.
   ☐ b. general reference map.
   ☐ c. population map.

3. The map that would tell if it rained the day you were born would be

   ☐ a. a weather map.
   ☐ b. an annual rainfall map.
   ☐ c. a climate map.

4. On the climate map of a continent, one thing you can find out just by looking at the legend is

   ☐ a. where each climate region is on the continent.
   ☐ b. how many climate regions there are on the continent.
   ☐ c. how large each climate region on the continent is.

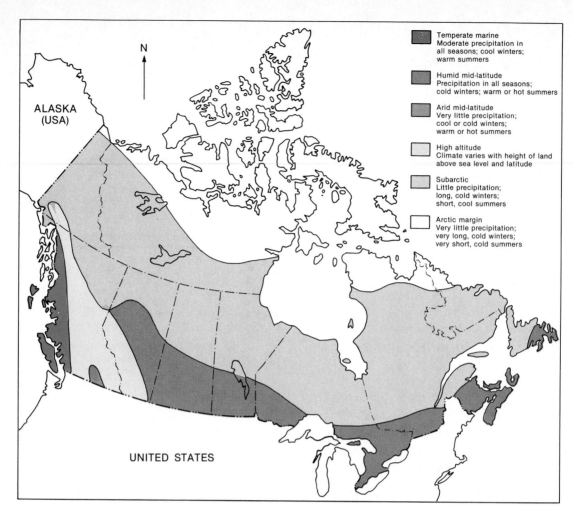

Figure 13.4 CANADA: CLIMATE REGIONS

B. Use Figures 13.4 and 13.5 to complete the following statements.

1. (a) The map in Figure 13.4 shows the _____ regions in Canada.

   (b) The number of regions shown on that map is _____ .

   (c) The map in Figure 13.5 is a _____ map of Canada.

2. (a) The name of the climate region that is farthest north in Canada is

   _____ .

   (b) In that region, the temperature is _____ all year long.

   (c) The number of people per square mile in that region is _____ .

3. (a) _____ is the name of the climate region where most of the people

   in Canada live.

   (b) The temperature in that region ranges from _____ in summer to

   _____ in winter.

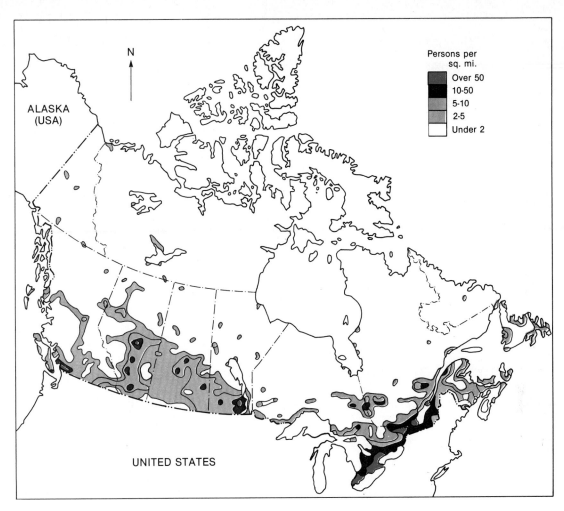

Figure 13.5 CANADA: POPULATION DISTRIBUTION

4. (a) Per square mile, there are _____ people in the south part of Canada than in the north part.

(b) It is probably because it is so _____ in the _____ part of Canada that fewer people live there.

Check your answers on page 138.

> Look back at **How Much Do You Already Know?** on page 118. Did you complete each statement correctly? If not, can you do so now?

This quiz will help you find out if you have learned the material covered in Chapters 7 through 13.

A. Tell which of the following statements are true and which are false.

1. The most important latitude line is the prime meridian. _____

2. Both sizes and shapes of land and water areas are shown accurately by the Mercator projection. _____

3. Every map projection causes distortion of some sort. _____

4. The Mollweide projection shows the true sizes of land and water areas. _____

5. The most accurate way to locate places on a map is by latitude and longitude. _____

6. A map scale expressed as a representative fraction could look like this: 1:1,000,000. _____

7. The imaginary line at 40°N is a longitude line. _____

8. A climate map shows information about the weather in a region for a particular day. _____

9. Lines, colors, patterns, words, and symbols are all part of map language. _____

10. A map scale shows how distances on a map compare to distances on the earth's surface. _____

Quiz 2
Maps

B. Match each term with its definition.

____ 1. symbol

____ 2. legend

____ 3. weather map

____ 4. road map

____ 5. atlas

____ 6. cartographer

____ 7. contour line

____ 8. index

____ 9. mean temperature

____ 10. precipitation

a. a book of maps

b. the part of a map that explains symbols

c. map language

d. a list that tells where cities and towns are on a map

e. one kind of general reference map

f. hail, mist, rain, sleet, or snow

g. a picture on a map that stands for something

h. an isoline that shows altitude

i. one kind of special purpose map

j. a person who makes maps

k. the average of several temperatures

C. Use the map and inset in Figure 1 to answer the questions at the top of page 130.

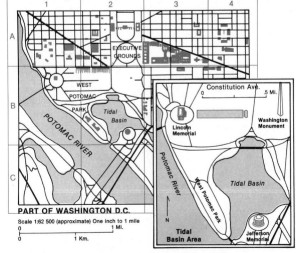

Figure 1   Washington, D.C.

1. Which grid squares on the map show the part of Washington that is blown up in the inset of the Tidal Basin Area? _____

2. Which has the larger scale, the map of Washington or the inset of the Tidal Basin Area? _____

3. What kind of map scale does the inset have? _____

4. In miles, about how far is it from the Jefferson Memorial to the Lincoln Memorial?

   _____

5. Which direction is it from the Washington Monument to the Lincoln Memorial?

   _____

Figure 2 Australia: Land Use

D. Use Figures 2 and 3 to answer the following questions.

1. According to the land use map, how many different types of land use are there in Australia? _____

2. According to the maps, what kind of land are sheep and cattle raised on in Australia? _____

3. Why does it make sense that sheep and cattle are raised where they are in Australia? _____

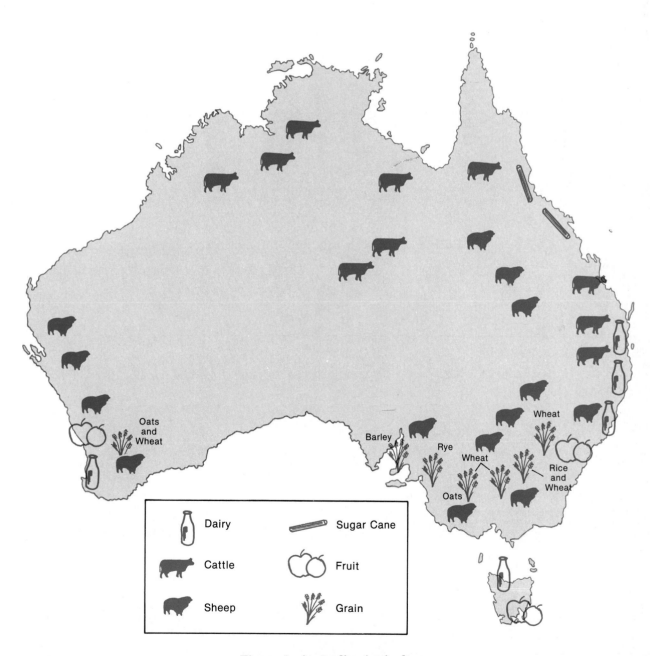

Figure 3 Australia: Agriculture

4. According to the maps, what three crops are grown on the cultivated land near

Perth? _____ , _____ , and _____

5. What is the likely reason that there is no agriculture in the area northeast of Perth?

_____

Check your answers on page 138.

Do You Need to Review?

The following chart shows the numbers of all the items in Quiz 2. You can use it to find which chapter you should review for any item you missed.

	Part A	Part B	Part C	Part D
Chapter 7	2, 3, 4	5		
Chapter 8	1, 5, 7	8	5	
Chapter 9	9	1, 2, 6, 7		
Chapter 10	6, 10		2, 3, 4	
Chapter 11		9, 10		1, 4
Chapter 12			1	
Chapter 13	8	3, 4		2, 3, 5

Glossary

The numbers in parentheses indicate the chapter in which each term is first used in this book.

atlas (7) A book of maps and related information

cardinal directions (3) North, south, east, and west

cartographer (9) Mapmaker

cold front (11) The leading edge of a mass of cold air that overtakes and passes under a warm air mass, usually causing showers or snow

continent (1) One of the seven great land masses on earth; in order of size, largest first: Asia, Africa, North America, South America, Antarctica, Europe, Australia

contour line (9) On a map, an isoline that shows altitude

equator (2) An imaginary line that runs around the middle of the earth (the latitude line at 0°); all north and south measurements are made from this line

general reference map (13) A map that shows several kinds of features and gives various types of information, such as a road map

globe (1) A scale model of the earth with the shape of a ball

graphic scale (10) A map scale that looks something like a ruler

Example:

gridpoint (8) On a map or a globe, the place where a latitude line crosses a longitude line

grid square (8) On a map that has a grid system for use in locating places, one of the squares in that system; usually identified by a letter and a number, such as **B5**

grid system (8) On a map, usually a pattern of small squares used for locating places

hemisphere (2) Half of the earth's surface

index (8) On a map, an alphabetical list of cities and towns that tells where they are located on the map

inset (12) A small map that blows up part of the area on a larger map to show it in more detail

intermediate directions (3) NE, SE, SW, and NW. The directions between the cardinal directions.

International Date Line (5) The meridian at 180°, halfway around the globe from the prime meridian

interrupted projection (7) A Mollweide projection with the water areas cut up to correct distortions in the shapes of land areas; also called *broken projection*

isoline (9) On a map, a line that shows all the places where the temperature, rainfall, altitude, or some other condition is the same (See CONTOUR LINE and ISOTHERM.)

isotherm (9) On a map, an isoline that shows temperature

kilometer (6) A measure of distance equal to about 0.6 miles

large-scale map (10) A map that shows an area, usually small, with a lot of detail, such as a map with an RF of 1:62,500

latitude line (4) An imaginary line that runs east-west around the earth parallel to the equator; used to measure distances from the equator; also called PARALLEL.

legend (9) On a map, the key that explains the meanings of the symbols used on the map

longitude line (4) An imaginary line that runs north-south around the earth, passing through both poles; used to measure distances from the prime meridian; also called MERIDIAN

map (1) A two-dimensional drawing of all or part of the earth

map scale (10) A drawing or other expression that shows how distances on a map or globe relate to distances on the earth. (See GRAPHIC SCALE, REPRESENTATIVE FRACTION, and WORDS AND FIGURES SCALE.)

mean temperature (11) The average of several temperatures recorded over a period of time

Mercator projection (7) A map projection that is good for telling directions even though it distorts the sizes, but not the shapes, of land and water areas

meridian (4) (See LONGITUDE LINE.)

Mollweide projection (7) An oval map projection that is good for telling sizes of land and water areas, even though it distorts their shapes; also called *equal area projection*

North Pole (2) The point through which all longitude lines run at the very top of a globe, 90° north of the equator

parallel (4) (See LATITUDE LINE.)

precipitation (11) Hail, mist, rain, sleet, or snow

prime meridian (3) An imaginary line that runs from the North Pole to the South Pole through Greenwich, England (the longitude line at 0°); all east and west measurements are made from this line.

projection (7) A system by which the features of the globe are represented on a flat map (See INTERRUPTED PROJECTION, MERCATOR PROJECTION, and MOLLWEIDE PROJECTION.)

representative fraction (10) A map scale that compares one unit of measure on a map to a number of equal units on the earth's surface; common abbreviation: RF; example: 1:62,500

small-scale map (10) A map that shows an area, usually large, in little detail, such as a map with an RF of 1:1,000,000

South Pole (2) The point through which all longitude lines run at the very bottom of a globe, 90° south of the equator.

special purpose map (13) A map that shows one kind of feature or gives information about one topic, such as an annual rainfall map

symbol (9) On a map, a shape or picture that stands for something; example: ✈ could stand for airport.

time zone (5) An area of the world where all places are on the same time; the world is divided into twenty-four time zones.

warm front (11) The leading edge of a mass of warm air that passes over and displaces a cold air mass, usually causing warm, wet weather

words and figures scale (10) A map scale expressed in words and numbers; example: 1 inch = 500 miles

Answer Key

Chapter 1 Globes and Maps

How Much Do You Already Know? (p. 2)

1. b
2. a
3. a
4. c

How Carefully Did You Read? (p. 7)

A.

1. b
2. b
3. c
4. a

B.

A. Arctic Ocean
B. North America
C. Europe
D. Asia
E. Atlantic Ocean
F. Africa
G. Pacific Ocean
H. South America
I. Indian Ocean
J. Australia
K. Antarctica

Chapter 2 Features of a Globe

How Much Do You Already Know? (p. 10)

1. a
2. b
3. c
4. a

How Carefully Did You Read? (p. 15)

A.

1. b
2. b
3. c
4. a
5. a
6. a

B.

1. Southern
2. Northern
3. Asia
4. Africa
5. north
6. Eastern; Northern
7. North America; South America
8. Africa; South America

Chapter 3 Directions on a Globe

How Much Do You Already Know? (p. 18)

1. a
2. a
3. c
4. b

How Carefully Did You Read? (p. 23)

A.

1. b
2. b
3. b
4. a
5. c
6. c

B.

1. eighteen (18)
2. Florida
3. North Carolina
4. Kansas
5. Virginia
6. Arkansas; Louisiana
7. Alabama; Georgia
8. southeast
9. northeast
10. southeast
11. northwest

Chapter 4 Locating Places on a Globe

How Much Do You Already Know? (p. 26)

1. a
2. c
3. b
4. c

How Carefully Did You Read? (p. 31)

A.

1. c
2. b
3. a
4. c
5. c
6. a
7. c

B.

1. 30°S
2. North Pole
3. 60°W
4. 30°S; 60°S
5. 60°N 30°E
6. C
7. D
8. 60°S 120°W

Chapter 5 Longitude and Time Zones

How Much Do You Already Know? (p. 34)

1. a
2. c
3. c
4. b

How Carefully Did You Read? (p. 41)

A.

1. c
2. a
3. b
4. c
5. a
6. c
7. c

B.

1. 1:00 P.M.
2. 8:00 P.M.
3. 7:00 A.M.
4. earlier
5. 1:00 P.M.
6. 3:00 A.M.
7. 2:00 A.M.
8. later
9. five
10. midnight

Chapter 6 Finding Distances on a Globe

How Much Do You Already Know? (p. 44)

1. a
2. a
3. c
4. a

How Carefully Did You Read? (p. 50)

A.

1. b
2. c
3. b
4. c
5. b

B.

1. 2,450
2. 6,000
3. 1,587
4. 207
5. 1,035

Quiz 1: Globes (p. 52)

A.

1. True
2. False
3. False
4. False
5. True
6. False
7. True
8. True
9. True
10. True

B.

1. d
2. b
3. a
4. c

C.

1. North Pole
2. latitude lines (parallels)
3. prime meridian
4. equator
5. longitude lines (meridians)
6. South Pole

D.

1. equator
2. continents
3. North America; South America
4. Northern
5. Southern
6. Western
7. Eastern
8. Answers will vary. Sample answer: North America; Northern; Western

E.

1. 2 inches
2. 69 miles
3. your friend

F.

1. southeast
2. Mexico
3. 690 miles
4. 10°N 70°W
5. C

Chapter 7 Map Projections

How Much Do You Already Know? (p. 58)

1. c
2. a
3. b
4. c

How Carefully Did You Read? (p. 64)

A.

1. b
2. a
3. b
4. a
5. b
6. c

B. Answers will vary. Sample answers:

1. Advantage: Maps are good for telling directions. Disadvantage: Sizes of land and water areas are distorted.
2. Advantage: Maps are good for comparing sizes of land and water areas. Disadvantage: Shapes of land and water areas are distorted.
3. Advantage: Sizes of land and water areas are accurate, and shapes are distorted only a little. Disadvantage: Water areas are distorted by being cut up.

Chapter 8 Locating Places on a Map

How Much Do You Already Know? (p. 66)

1. a
2. b
3. b
4. b

How Carefully Did You Read? (p. 73)

A.

1. a
2. c
3. b
4. c
5. b

B.

1. 30°N 110°W
2. Alaska
3. 40°N
4. 70°N 50°W

5. Miami, Florida
6. Mexico
7. 35°N 130°W
8. San Jose, Costa Rica

C.

1. Pierre, South Dakota
2. Boise, Idaho
3. Helena, Montana
4. Wichita, Kansas
5. Bismarck, North Dakota
6. Carson City, Nevada, or Sacramento, California

D.

1. G9   4. G2
2. H9   5. D2
3. H13

Chapter 9   Map Language

How Much Do You Already Know? (p. 76)

1. b   3. a
2. c   4. b

How Carefully Did You Read? (p. 83)

A.

1. c   4. b
2. a   5. b
3. a

B.

1. b   4. a
2. c   5. c
3. c   6. c

C.

1. Military Trail
2. five (5)
3. St. Mary's Hospital
4. (a) Lake Magnolia Boulevard, or Rt. 702
   (b) Australian Avenue
   (c) Broadway, or Rt. A1A
5. (a) Belvedere Road
   (b) Southern Boulevard, or Rt. 80
6. a town

Chapter 10   Map Scales

How Much Do You Already Know? (p. 88)

1. b   3. a
2. b   4. c

How Carefully Did You Read? (p. 95)

A.

1. c   5. b
2. c   6. c
3. c   7. c
4. b   8. a

B.

1. 300 miles
2. 320 kilometers
3. 45 miles; 75 kilometers
4. 27 miles; 45 kilometers
5. 33 miles; 52 kilometers
6. 30 miles
7. 1 mile
8. 1:1,000,000

Chapter 11   Legends

How Much Do You Already Know? (p. 98)

1. a   3. c
2. b   4. c

How Carefully Did You Read? (p. 105)

A.

1. b   3. b
2. a   4. c

B.

1. less than 10; 80 inches and over
2. less than 10
3. 40–60
4. 20–40

C.

1. 10°F
2. 70°F
3. flurries; snow
4. cold
5. sunny; 60
6. cloudy; 20

Chapter 12   Map Insets

How Much Do You Already Know? (p. 110)

1. b   3. b
2. a   4. b

How Carefully Did You Read? (p. 115)

A.

1. b   3. a
2. a   4. c

B.

1. Philadelphia; Central Philadelphia
2. Answers will vary, but the map and inset both have these features: I-676, I-95, Route 611, J. F. Kennedy Blvd., Market Street, Walnut Street, 10th St., 7th St., 5th St., Front St., the Delaware River, and others.
3. 3
4. $\frac{1}{3}$
5. C2; C3

Chapter 13   Special Purpose Maps

How Much Do You Already Know? (p. 118)

1. b   3. c
2. a   4. b

How Carefully Did You Read?
(p. 125)

A.

1. b   3. a
2. a   4. b

B.

1. (a) climate
   (b) six (6)
   (c) population
2. (a) Arctic Margin
   (b) cold
   (c) less than 2
3. (a) Humid mid-latitude
   (b) hot; cold
4. (a) more
   (b) cold; north

Quiz 2: Maps (p. 128)

A.

1. False   6. True
2. False   7. False
3. True   8. False
4. True   9. True
5. True   10. True

B.

1. g   6. j
2. b   7. h
3. i   8. d
4. e   9. k
5. a   10. f

C.

1. B1 and B2

2. the inset of the Tidal Basin Area
3. a graphic scale
4. one (1) mile
5. west

D.

1. four (4)
2. grassland
3. The form of answers will vary, but they should express this idea: Sheep and cattle graze, or feed, on grass, so grassland is a good place to raise them.
4. oats, wheat, and fruit
5. The form of answers will vary, but they should express this idea: That area is a desert, so no animals or crops could be raised there.